Jake Wright

OCR A2 Computing
F453 Advanced Computing Theory

Revision Guide

Every effort has been made to trace copyright holders and to obtain their permission for the use of copyright material. The author will gladly receive information enabling him to rectify any reference or credit in subsequent editions.

First published 2012

http://jakewright.net

Copyright © 2012 Jake Wright

ISBN 978-1-4949-6013-1

All rights reserved. No part of this publication may be reproduced, distributed, or transmitted in any form or by any means, including photocopying, recording, or other electronic or mechanical methods, without the prior written permission of the copyright owner.

Edited by Eszter Soós

CONTENTS

Chapter 1 The Function of Operating Systems 1
    1.1 Interrupts 1
    1.2 Scheduling 2
    1.3 Memory Management 5
    1.4 Spooling 7
    1.5 Modern Operating Systems 8

Chapter 2 The Function and Purpose of Translators 10
    2.1 Assembly Language and Assemblers 11
    2.2 Compilation and Interpretation 12
    2.3 Stages of Compilation 13
    2.4 Virtual Machines and Intermediate Code 18
    2.5 Library Routines 19

Chapter 3 Computer Architectures 20
    3.1 Von Neumann Architecture 20
    3.2 Co-Processors 21
    3.3 Parallel Processing 22
    3.4 RISC and CISC 22

Chapter 4 Data Representation 23
    4.1 Expressing Real Numbers in Binary 23
    4.2 Negative Numbers in Binary 23
    4.3 Floating point Binary 25

Chapter 5 Data Structures and Data Manipulation 27
    5.1 Data Structures 27
    5.2 Sorting Algorithms 31
    5.3 Searching Algorithms 34
    5.4 Merging Data 35

Chapter 6 High-Level Language Programming Paradigms 36
6.1 Low vs. High-Level Languages 36
6.2 Procedural Languages 36
6.3 Declarative Languages 36
6.4 Object-Oriented Programming 37

Chapter 7 Programming Techniques 44
7.1 Stepwise Refinement 44
7.2 Standard Programming Techniques 44
7.3 Backus-Naur Form (BNF) 45
7.4 Syntax Diagrams 46
7.5 Reverse Polish Notation 47

Chapter 8 Low-Level Languages 49
8.1 Memory Addressing 49

Chapter 9 Databases 52
9.1 Flat Files Databases 52
9.2 Relational Databases 53
9.3 Database Normalisation 55
9.4 Primary, Secondary and Foreign Keys 56
9.5 Database Views 56
9.6 Database Management Systems 57

Appendix 1 Index 58

CHAPTER 1 THE FUNCTION OF OPERATING SYSTEMS

The operating system must:

- Provide and manage hardware resources (e.g. memory)
- Provide an interface between the user and the machine
- Provide an interface between hardware and software
- Provide security for the data on the system
- Provide utility software to maintain the system

1.1 INTERRUPTS

Interrupts are messages sent to the processor to obtain processor time. Each interrupt has a priority. There are different types of interrupt:

I/O Interrupt
Generated by an I/O device to signal that a job is complete or an error has occurred, e.g. printer is out of paper.

Timer Interrupt
Generated by an internal clock indicating that the processor must attend to time critical activities.

Hardware Error
E.g. power failure (which would have the highest priority of all interrupts).

Program Interrupt
Generated due to an error in a program, e.g. attempting to divide by zero.

Interrupts are held in a **queue**. After each CPU cycle, the queue is checked for an interrupt with a higher priority than the current job. **If an interrupt with a higher priority is found, the contents of the registers are put on a stack. This allows the job to resume once the interrupt has been processed.**

Remember, the CPU registers include the PC, CIR, MAR, MDR and Accumulator.

Once all higher priority interrupts have been processed, the contents of registers are pulled from the stack and the original job is resumed.

By placing the contents of the registers on a stack, the problem caused by an interrupt occurring during the processing of another interrupt is solved. Remember, a stack is a last-in-first-out "LIFO" data structure.

Stack

Higher Priority Interrupt
Interrupt
Original Task

1.2 SCHEDULING

The OS must arrange jobs that need to be done into an appropriate order. The objectives of scheduling are to:

- **Maximise the use** of the computer system
- Be **fair** to all users
- Provide a **reasonable response time** to all users
- **Prevent the system failing** if it's becoming overloaded
- Ensure that the system is **consistent** by always giving similar response times to similar activities from day to day

The following criteria may influence the order in which jobs are executed:

- The **priority** of a job
- **I/O or processor** bound (see below)
- The **type** of job, i.e. batch processing or real-time
- **Resource requirement**, e.g. the amount of time needed to complete a job, memory required
- Resources used so far
- **How long** the job has been waiting

A JOB CAN BE I/O BOUND OR PROCESSOR BOUND

I/O Bound
Suppose Program A prints wage slips for the employees of a company. This program will make little use of the processor because the calculations are small whereas it needs a lot of printing and has to get lots of data from disk drives. Because most of the things that this job does concern input and output, this job is called an I/O bound job.

Processor Bound
Program B, however, may analyse the annual, world-wide sales of the company, which has a turnover of many millions of pounds and will therefore make a great deal of use of the processor, only needing to collect one set of data from the drive and producing one lot of printout at the end. Jobs like this are said to be processor bound.

THE SCHEDULER

A job can only be in one of three states: **ready to start**, **running** or **blocked** (e.g. blocked because it is waiting for a peripheral).

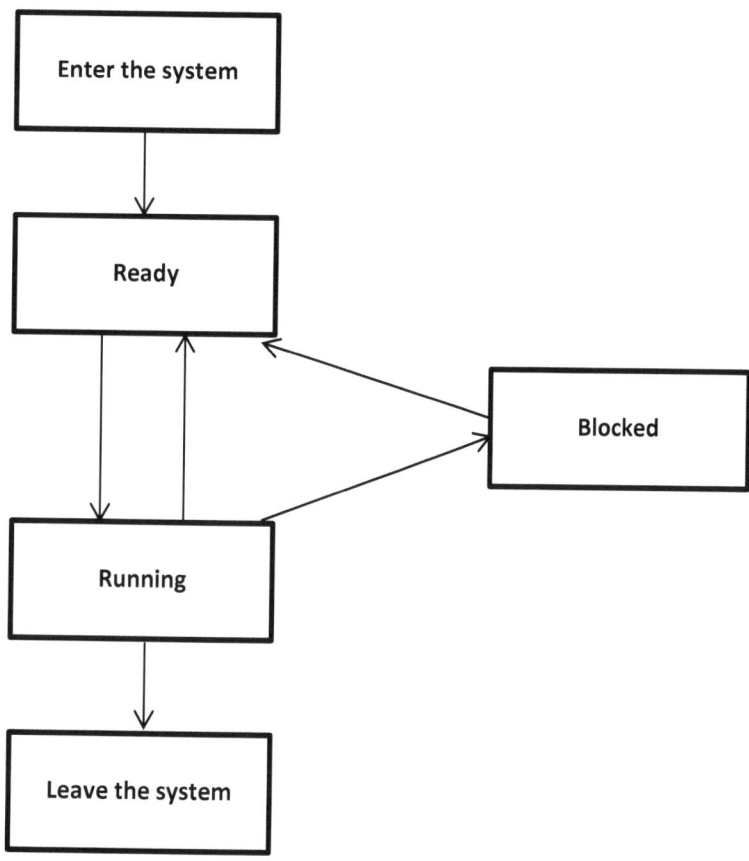

The **Scheduler** is a program used by the OS to control the jobs. There are different sections of the program: 'high level', 'medium level' and 'low level'.

- Jobs entering the system are placed in the ready queue by the **High Level Scheduler** (**HLS**). The HLS makes sure the system is not overloaded.
- Sometimes jobs must be swapped between main memory and the backing store. This is done by the **Medium Level Scheduler** (**MLS**).
- Moving jobs in and out of the ready state is done by the **Low Level Scheduler** (**LLS**). The LLS decides the order in which jobs are to be placed in the running state.

There are two types of scheduler:

- A **pre-emptive scheduler** will stop jobs that are currently running to make way for another job
- A **non-pre-emptive scheduler** will leave a job in the running state until it is finished, making other jobs wait

SCHEDULING ALGORITHMS

There are several different types of scheduling algorithms (also known as *scheduling policies*).

FCFS - First come, first served
The first job to enter the ready queue is the first to enter the running state. This favours long jobs because, once in the running state, there is nothing to stop them carrying on.

SJF – Shortest job first
The queue is sorted by expected execution time. New jobs are placed in the correct position in the queue.

RR – Round robin
Each job gets a maximum length of processor time (called a time slice) after which the job is put at the back of the ready queue and the next job gets its time slice.

SRT – Shortest remaining time
Similar to 'shortest job first' but jobs move further up the queue as they are processed. Long jobs may never be executed though, if they never get to the front of the queue.

MFQ – Multi-level feedback queues
Involves several queues with jobs moving downwards as they use more processing time. A job is given one chance to complete at a given queue level before it is forced down to a lower level. At the lowest level, a round robin system is used. See diagram below.

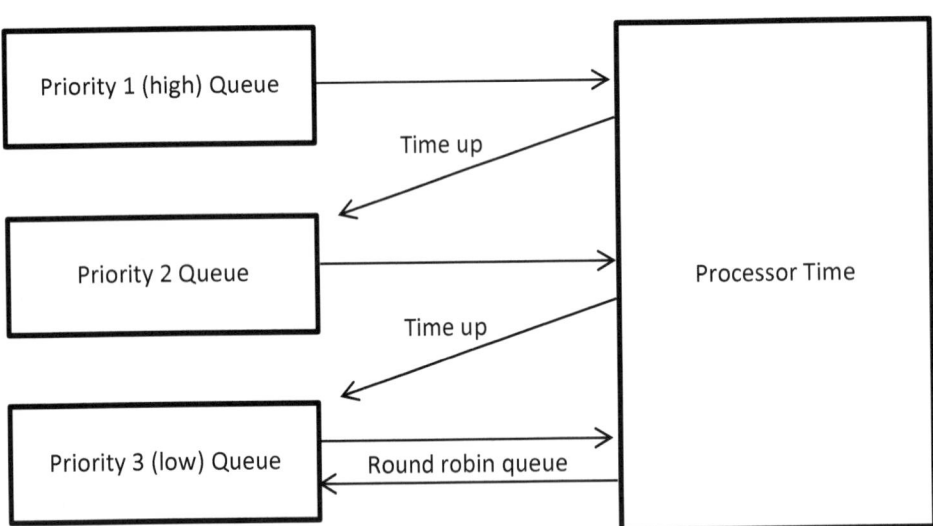

1.3 MEMORY MANAGEMENT

For a job to be able to use the processor, it must be stored in the computer's memory. The primary can be imagined as a stack:

Primary Memory
Free 20kB
Job D 30kB
Job C 10kB
Job B 20kB
Job A 50kB
OS (*remember that the OS will require some memory*)

The physical memory reserved for the operating system is called wired memory and is not subject to paging.

MEMORY MANAGEMENT IS NECESSARY TO:

- Allocate memory to allow **separate processes to run simultaneously**
- **Reallocate memory** when necessary
    - For example, when a job finishes and no longer needs memory
- Protect processes from each other
    - So a job cannot access the memory used by another job
    - So a job gets **exclusive** access to designated memory addresses
- Deal with <u>virtual memory, paging and segmentation</u> (see following sections)

In the stack above, suppose Job C terminates and Job E, which is in the ready queue, requires 25kB of memory. This job cannot fit in the free space, or in the space that Job C occupied, even though there is now 30kB of free space in total.

- You could **wait until a big enough gap is available**, but this could take a long time and would be a **waste of resources**.
- Job D could be **moved down** to create a section of memory big enough for Job E, however, this would make **heavy use of the processor** because all of the instructions would have to be moved down and all of the memory addresses would have to be recalculated.
- Job E could be **split** into two parts, storing one part where Job C was and the other in the free space, but this would cause **fragmentation** problems.

The following sections describe the solution to this problem.

VIRTUAL MEMORY

Virtual memory – giving the illusion of more physical memory than there really is.

The purpose of virtual memory is therefore to be the solution to not having enough physical memory.

Programs may store lots of instructions and data in memory at one time, but not all of it will be used simultaneously. Virtual memory takes advantage of this by splitting a program into blocks and only copying the blocks of a program and data that are actually being executed into primary memory.

Virtual memory introduces a **layer of abstraction** between program code and physical memory.
Virtual memory is like an alternate set of memory addresses.
Programs use these **virtual addresses** to store instructions and data.
When the program is executed, the virtual addresses are converted into real memory addresses.
The process of translating, or mapping, a virtual address into a physical address is called **virtual address translation**.

SOFTWARE	VIRTUAL MEMORY	PHYSICAL MEMORY
Programs wanting to store instructions and data in memory	Programs put their instructions and data here as though this is the primary memory. Virtual memory (since it's virtual and not limited by the physical size of the computer's RAM) will be big enough to accommodate everything that needs to be stored in memory.	Data in the virtual memory is copied to physical memory when it actually is executed. The virtual memory addresses are mapped to the physical memory addresses.

Arrows between boxes labelled "Virtual Address Translation".

A limited amount of data can be stored in physical memory

PAGE FILE AND DISK THRASHING

The sections of programs and data not currently being executed are normally stored on the *hard disk*. If the amount of data which actually needs to be stored in physical memory (because it's all being executed) exceeds the size of the physical memory, a lot of swapping of blocks occurs between the hard disk and the physical memory. This heavy disk usage is known as **disk thrashing**: pages are swapped in and out and then accessed quickly causing frequent faults. *(OCR call this threshing but they mean the same thing.)*

Remember, the hard disk is secondary storage and is considerably slower than the physical memory (RAM), which is primary storage.

PAGING AND SEGMENTATION

The instructions and data stored in virtual memory are split into blocks so only those that need executing can be copied to the physical memory. There are two ways of determining the size of these blocks: paging and segmentation.

PAGING

In the paging memory-management scheme, the data transferred between virtual memory and physical memory is split into **equally sized blocks** called pages.

The **index** keeps track of what is in each page.

Pages in virtual memory, that are not being executed, are stored on disk in a **page file**.

Page	Contents
1	
2	Job A
3	
4	
5	Job B
6	
7	
8	Job C
9	

Code is split over multiple pages

SEGMENTATION

Segmentation avoids the possibility of splitting up code halfway through a function, for example, because pages are not big enough. Segments are **adjustable size blocks**, i.e. the size of a segment is not fixed whereas the size of a page is.

A segment will hold an entire section of code, relying on **logical breaks** in the code.

Space is not wasted, as it would be in a page if the page size were bigger than the data going into it, and the code is not split as it would be if it were bigger than the page size.

Segments are also indexed.

1.4 SPOOLING

Spooling is the process of placing data in a temporary working area while waiting for another process to finish. The most common example is print spooling. A printer can only cope with one job at a time, so if multiple jobs are sent to the printer, the rest must be placed somewhere else until the printer is ready.

The jobs are stored in the temporary working area, usually the hard drive. References to where the jobs are stored are placed in the **spool queue**. It's an unusual queue that allows pushing in; jobs with a higher priority will be placed higher up the queue.

Spooling saves the user waiting for the printer (or other slow device) and allows the processor to do something else while the printing (or other slow process) finishes. (An interrupt would be sent to request the next job from the spool queue.)

1.5 MODERN OPERATING SYSTEMS

There are two main types of OS: **command line** and those with a **graphical user interface** (**GUI**, pronounced *gooey*).

- MS-DOS was a command line operating system
- Windows has a graphical user interface

Modern operating systems allow apparent multi-tasking by switching between multiple tasks very quickly. Each application gets a **time-slice**. When their processor time is up, an interrupt occurs and control is passed to the next application.

BOOT PROCESS

When the computer is first turned on, the **CPU initialises itself**.
Part of this initialisation is to look for the **BIOS** (Basic Input Output System).
Some of the BIOS is stored in ROM (read only memory), but since it is user-configurable, it is not completely stored in ROM; these parts are stored in CMOS RAM (random access memory).

> *CMOS (complementary metal-oxide semiconductor) is a type of memory chip with very low power requirements. Thanks to battery power, it retains data when the PC is turned off. The BIOS cannot be stored on the hard disk because it contains the code to initialise such secondary storage devices.*

The BIOS will then run its power-on-self-test.

Power-on-self-test (POST)
Firstly, the computer runs the power-on-self-test (POST) routine that is stored in ROM. The POST routine:

- Checks the BIOS chip and tests the CMOS RAM
- Verifies and clears CPU registers
- Checks hardware devices, e.g. video card, secondary storage devices, keyboard, mouse
- Loads the address of the first instruction of the ***boot program*** into the program counter (PC)

Boot Program
The boot program is also known as the boot loader, or the bootstrap, and is stored in ROM.
It looks for an OS to load.

 On a typical PC, the OS will be loaded from the 'C drive', but it will check the floppy drive and CD drive beforehand. The order in which devices are checked for an OS is called the **boot sequence**, and can be configured in the CMOS setup.

Once an OS has been located, the boot program will encounter the **boot record**, which tells it where to find the beginning of the OS and the subsequent program that will initialise the OS.

OS Initialisation
Once the program that initialises the OS is loaded, the BIOS copies its files into memory and the OS can take control over the rest of the boot process. The OS performs another check of the memory and loads the device **drivers** needed by peripherals such as printers, scanners, mice and keyboards.

FILE ALLOCATION TABLES (FAT)

The OS must be able to store and locate files on a disk. It uses a **File Allocation Table (FAT)** to do this.

File Allocation Table (FAT) is a computer file system architecture. FAT file systems are commonly found on devices such as floppy disks and flash memory cards. FAT was also commonly used on hard disks but its use has declined since Windows XP, which favoured the newer NTFS. There are many other file systems including HFS+ which is used by Mac OS X. The OCR spec requires knowledge of how an OS using the file system would use the actual file allocation table.

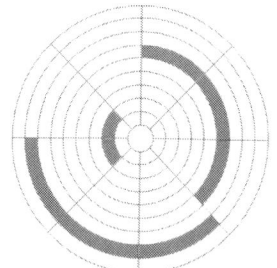

The FAT uses a **linked list** to point to the blocks on the disk that contain files. To do this, the OS formats the disk by dividing it into sectors and concentric circles (called tracks). Two or more sectors on a single track make up a cluster. The FAT is loaded into RAM to speed up the search time and to avoid continual disk access.

The diagram to the left will give you an idea of the structure of a hard drive. The shaded sectors represent clusters.

Below is an example of a file allocation table. Every cluster on the disk is listed. If the cluster is empty, it has a **zero entry**. Otherwise, the cluster containing the beginning of a file is labelled (with a **pointer**), and links to the cluster containing the next part of the file. The cluster containing the end of the file has a **null pointer**.

File Pointers	Cluster	Pointer
	1	0
file-1.jpg	2	3
	3	5
file-2.doc	4	6
	5	EOF
	6	7
	7	EOF

We can see that cluster 1 is empty. Our first example file begins in cluster 2, the next part is in cluster 3, and the final part of the file is in cluster 5. File 2 begins in cluster 4, followed by cluster 6 with the remaining bits of the file in cluster 7.

The fragmentation of files is caused by deleting files. Note that a file is never deleted from the physical disk; only the reference to it is removed from the FAT. Of course, when the disk is full it will be overwritten.

To **find a file**, the OS looks in the table for the filename and, if it finds it, **gets the cluster number** for the start of the file. The OS can then **follow the pointers** in the table to find the rest of the file.

To **delete** a file, it just has to **set the clusters it occupied to zero**.

To **add a new file**, the OS has to **linearly search** for clusters with zero entries **to set up the linked list**.

CHAPTER 2 THE FUNCTION AND PURPOSE OF TRANSLATORS

A translator converts **source code** into **object code** (also known as machine code).

- Computers work with binary
- Humans find it difficult to read and write instructions in binary
- They prefer to write in higher level languages
- Something must convert the code written by programmers into the code the computer can understand

Source code is the original code written by the programmer. *This would be the code you write in Visual Basic.* A translator will convert this source code into object code, which is the binary that the computer can execute.

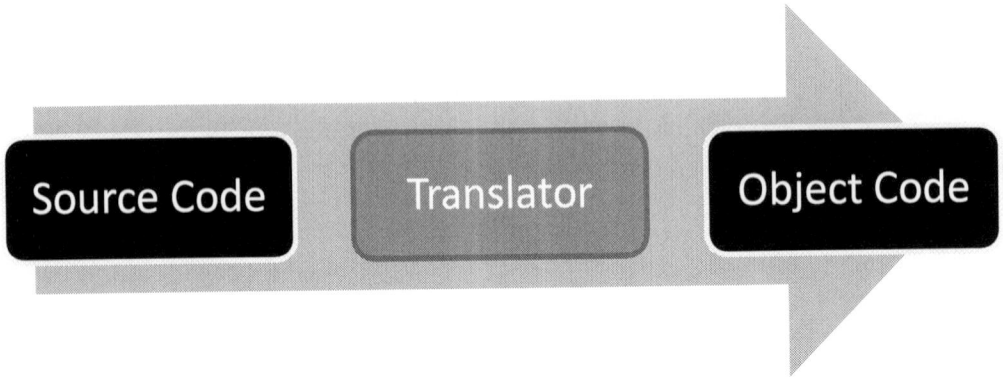

In the early days of computers, binary was the only way to program a computer. This was very difficult and, as programs became more complicated, so did the binary required to create them. This is why translators are required; **they let humans work with languages that are more abstract**.

There are 3 main types of translator that will be discussed in the following sections:

- **Compiler**
- **Interpreter**
- **Assembler**

Using intermediate code with a virtual machine is an alternative to separate compilation or interpretation.

2.1 ASSEMBLY LANGUAGE AND ASSEMBLERS

An assembly language is a low-level language with a one-to-one relationship with machine code (opcodes). An assembler translates an assembly language into object code.

An **opcode** is a particular binary operation that a computer can carry out, e.g. addition, multiplication.

In an assembly language, opcodes are represented by key words called **mnemonics** e.g. ADD, SUB or MULT. Mnemonics are stored in a **lookup table**. Similarly, memory addresses are given symbolic names called **labels**.

Opcode	Mnemonic
001	ADD
010	SUB
011	GET

Memory Address	Label
00100	NUM1
00101	NUM2
00110	NUM3

Writing code in mnemonics is easier than using raw binary.

Because every mnemonic is mapped directly to a single opcode, an assembly language has a **one-to-one relationship** with the binary. An assembly language is therefore specific to a certain computer architecture.

> **The assembly language and assembler are specific to a particular computer**

To execute a program written in an assembly language (the source code), it needs translating to the equivalent binary (object code). This is done by an **assembler**.

It's easy for an assembler to translate mnemonics because of the one-to-one-relationship:

- The lookup table is used to convert mnemonics to opcodes

Translating the labels is more complicated:

- The memory addresses that will be available to a program cannot be known before execution
- A lookup table therefore **cannot** exist to convert labels to memory addresses
- A table called a symbol table is created dynamically each time the program runs

Assembly Language
- Low-level language
- Uses mnemonics to represent opcodes (binary operations)
- Specific to machine architecture

Assembler
- Translates the assembly language into object code
- Converts mnemonics to opcodes using a lookup table
- Resolves symbolic names (labels) for memory locations and creates a symbol table

Object Code
- The raw binary that can be executed by the processor

2.2 COMPILATION AND INTERPRETATION

Compilers and interpreters both translate high-level programming languages into object code.

- A high-level language is **more abstract** than an assembly language.
    - It is less like machine code **and more like English**.
- A high-level language is more portable than an assembly language.
    - A program written in a high-level language can run on many different machines.
- **FORTRAN** is the earliest example of a high-level language.
    - Visual Basic is another example of a high-level programming language.
- A high-level language uses **keywords**, e.g. PRINT, FIND.
    - A keyword may have many lower layers of code, eventually linking to a series of machine code instructions.
    - They have a one-to-many relationship with machine code.
- Since a high-level language does **not** have a simple one-to-one relationship with machine language, an assembler is no good for translation.
    - There are two ways to translate a high-level language: compilation and interpretation.

COMPILERS

A compiler translates a program's source code into object code as a single unit.

- **All of the source code** is translated into object code before execution.
- A compiler will output an **executable** file (.exe in Windows).
- Once the program is compiled, it can **run without further help** from the compiler.
- The code can run very **quickly** because **translation only happens once**.
- Compilation is useful for **distributing** a program:
    - No need to distribute source code
    - Machine code is difficult to understand
    - Intellectual property is protected.
- However, **more memory** is needed to hold all of the object code and the compiler in memory at once.

INTERPRETERS

An interpreter translates a program's source code one line at a time.

- **Each line is translated and executed** before moving onto the next.
- Interpretation was developed because early **computers lacked the memory needed for compilation**.
    - Interpretation **uses less memory** – only one line loaded in memory at a time.
- **Error messages** are produced as soon as an error is encountered.
- Interpretation is useful for programmers when debugging (stepping through code in Visual Studio uses interpretation) because the programmer will know exactly **where the error occurred**.
- **A Translator must be present** in order to execute the code.
- The program will run **more slowly** because each line needs translating during execution.
- Instructions inside a loop will have to be **translated each time the loop is entered**.
- **Source code must be distributed** so it is harder to protect algorithms, etc.

2.3 STAGES OF COMPILATION

A parser is a component of a compiler. Parsing means to analyse the code.

There are three phases of compilation:

1. Lexical analysis
2. Syntax analysis
3. Code generation and optimisation

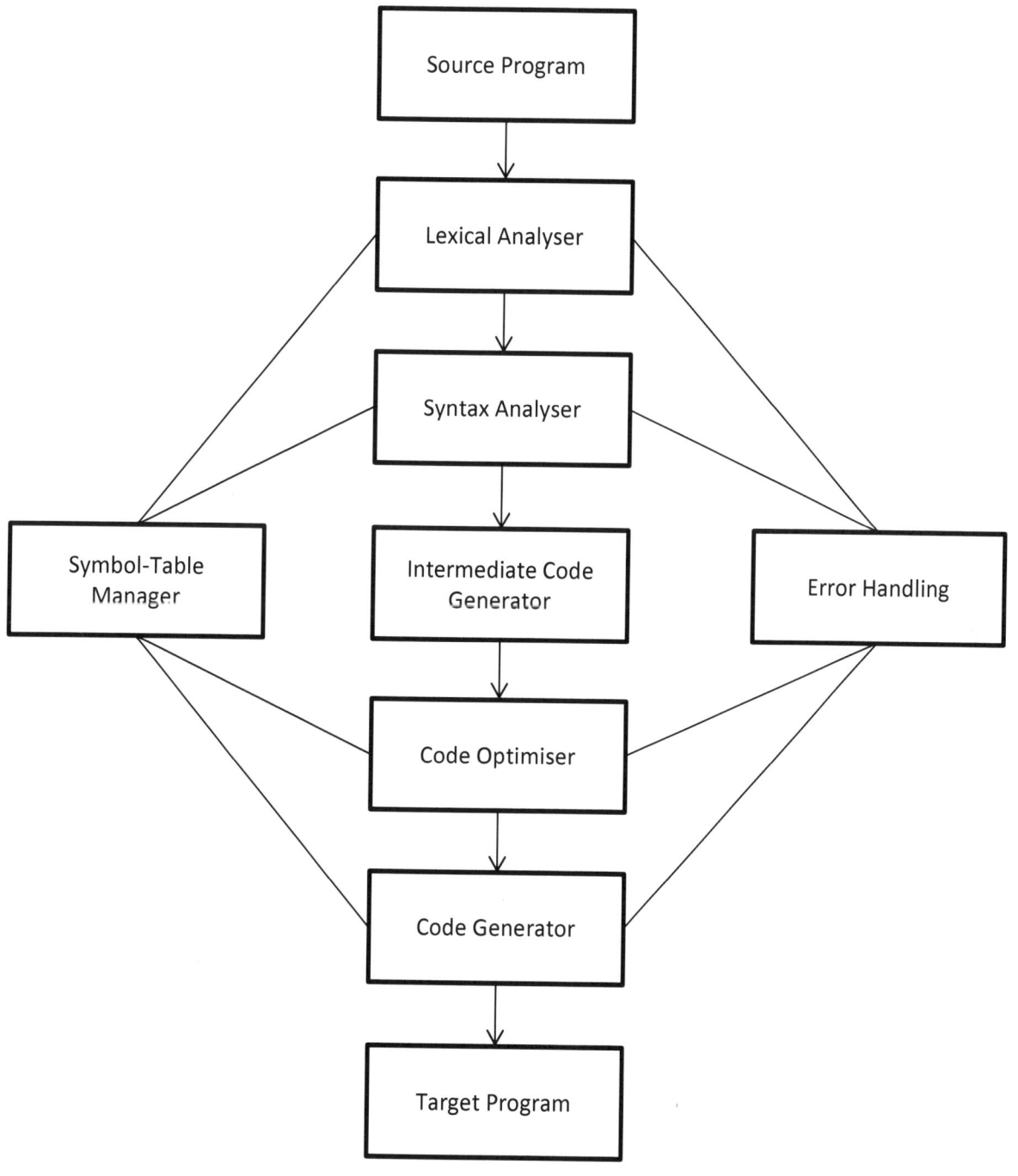

LEXICAL ANALYSIS

The lexical analyser uses the source program as input. It turns the code into a stream of tokens.

1. All comments and whitespace are **removed**.
2. Some **simple error checking** is performed. The analyser will report the following errors:
    a. An illegal or **unrecognised keyword** is used, i.e. characters that are not valid tokens
    b. An attempt to assign an **illegal value** to a constant
        e.g. `Const Name = Jake Wright` (the name should be in quotes)
    c. An identifier or constant is **too long** (as determined by the rules of the language).
3. **Tokens** are created from the input characters.
4. Identifiers (variable names) are placed in a **symbol table**.

TOKENISATION

Sets of related input characters form tokens. *Tokens are symbolic representations of the input characters.* Tokens are usually represented by numbers.
A specific group of characters that represent a token is called the **lexeme**.

E.g. suppose the input characters from the source code are:

`numberOfTiles = 4 * (width * height)`.

The following table of tokens and corresponding lexemes may be constructed:

Lexeme	Token Type
numberOfTiles	IDENTIFIER
=	OPERATOR_EQUALS
4	NUMBER
*	OPERATOR_MULT
(	L_BRACKET
width	IDENTIFIER
*	OPERATOR_MULT
height	IDENTIFIER
)	R_BRACKET

Each token would then be represented by a number and passed back to the parser for the next stage of compilation.

A **pattern** is a **rule** that a lexical analyser follows to create a token.

Patterns are normally defined by **regular expressions**, e.g. [a-z][a-zA-Z0-9]* may define an IDENTIFIER token type. This expression will recognise any lexeme with at least one alphanumeric letter, whose first letter is lower-case alphabetic.

Lexical analysis is the slowest phase of compilation because it deals with code in its most abstract form.

SYNTAX ANALYSIS

The code generated by the lexical analyser is checked to see that it is 'grammatically' correct.

Syntax analysis is the process of determining whether the sequence of input characters, symbols, items and tokens **form a valid sequence** in the language as defined by **BNF** or syntax diagrams.

E.g. the programming language may define a variable type STAFF_CODE using BNF as follows.

```
<DIGIT>      ::= 0|1|2|3|4|5|6|7|8|9
<LETTER>     ::= A|B|C|D|E
<STAFF_CODE> ::= <LETTER><DIGIT>|<STAFF_CODE><DIGIT>
```

The syntax analyser will make sure a variable of type STAFF_CODE is valid using the definition above.

During syntax analysis, certain **semantic** checks are carried out:

- Label checks – *make sure the line that a 'GOTO' statement passes control to exists*
- Flow of control checks – *make sure statements are used in the correct place and order e.g. CONTINUE can only be placed inside of a loop, IF statement matched with correct END IF*
- Declaration checks – *make sure all variables have been properly declared*

> Semantic means relating to meaning in language or logic. Something may be syntactically correct but semantically meaningless. 'Jake ate a banana' has meaning and obeys the rules of English but 'A banana ate Jake' obeys the rules but not the semantics.

*Note: although semantic checks check the logic to a certain extent, it is **not** the same as checking for a **logic error**. Remember, a logic error will not cause the program to crash; it will simply cause unexpected results. A compiler cannot find such errors.*

An example of a **logic error** is if the programmer has written $a = b + c$ instead of $a = b - c$.

CODE GENERATION AND OPTIMISATION

This is the final phase of compilation, where the code is optimised and the machine code is generated.

- Memory is allocated to variables as the identifiers are encountered during code generation
- The memory addresses are stored in the symbol table
- The lookup table is used to translate tokens into machine code

Intermediate code is produced before generating the final code. This intermediate code can be compiled into an executable file or interpreted by a virtual machine (discussed below).

This flowchart shows the two possible routes that can be taken when compiling source code written in a high-level language.

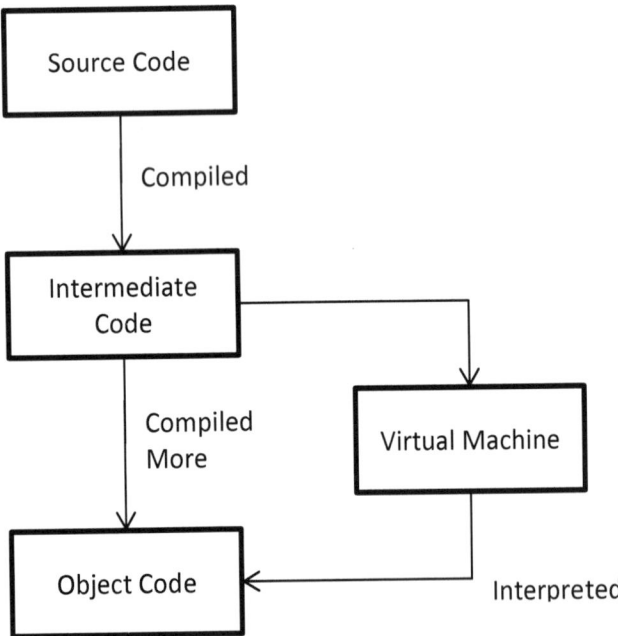

CODE OPTIMISATION

Once the code generator has created machine code, it tries to optimise the code to make it more efficient.

Consider the following lines of code.

```
x = y + 3
b = x
c = b
```

The code optimiser will **remove redundant code** so the above example could become:

```
c = y + 3.
```

A compiler's code optimiser can favour **speed** or **memory** optimisation because, in the real world, you often cannot optimise both.

THE SYMBOL TABLE

The symbol table is a data structure used by the compiler to store each identifier found in the source code.

It will contain an entry for every identifier along with information about each one:

- The **type** of item – *e.g. integer, real, char*
- The **scope** of the item – *local, global, etc.*
- The **memory address** holding the variable's value (or simply the **value** if it's a constant)

A simplified example of a symbol table:

Memory Address	Type	Identifier
00000010	Integer	width
00000011	String	username

As this table gets bigger, performing a linear search on it to find an identifier takes too long.

- The table is therefore commonly organised as a **hash table.**
- The position of an entry in the table is calculated by applying a **hashing algorithm** to the identifier.
- If two identifiers produce the same hash, a **linked list** is used.
    - The **synonym** (the identifier causing the collision) is put in the next available space and a pointer in the first space will link to its new location.
- *A symbol table may also be organised as a **binary tree**.*

2.4 VIRTUAL MACHINES AND INTERMEDIATE CODE

Using intermediate code is an alternative way to translate code written in a high-level language.

- Different computer architectures have different machine code
    - *001 may be the opcode for addition in one computer but subtraction in another*
- This means that they all need different compilers for each high-level language
    - *For example, if a program written in a high-level language is to run on 32-bit and 64-bit computers, it may need a separate compiler to make each version*
- An alternative is to use a compiler to create **intermediate code** which can run on a wider variety of architectures using a **virtual machine**
    - Source code is translated by a compiler to intermediate code *(known as **bytecode**)*
    - Intermediate code is half-way between source code and object code
        - It's closer to machine language but it is not machine specific
        - It's still an abstract language that needs further translation
    - The intermediate code can be distributed to a variety of platforms where it is interpreted by a virtual machine specific to each platform

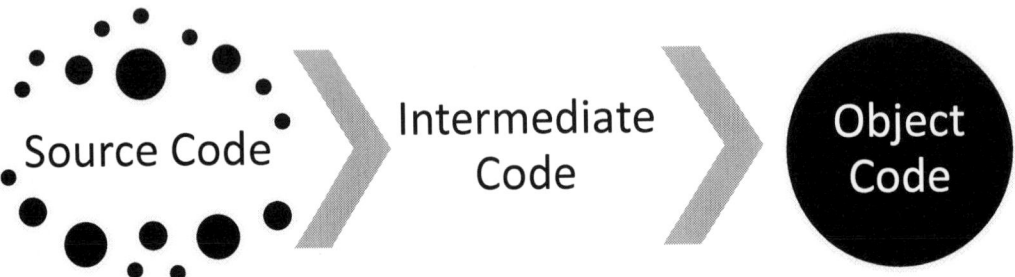

Programmer writes source code in high-level language

Source code is compiled to intermediate code

Virtual machine interprets intermediate code

WHY USE INTERMEDIATE CODE?

- Intermediate code can **run on a variety of computers**
    - It **improves portability** between machines
    - It means a programmer does not have to worry about compiling their code for every platform because the virtual machines (created by other people) will handle the final translation automatically
- The **same intermediate code can be obtained from different high-level languages**
    - Sections of a program can be written in **different languages**

A program running in a virtual machine will **run more slowly** than fully-compiled executable code because it has to be interpreted each time it is run.

Java is an example of a language that uses intermediate code. Java applications are compiled to bytecode (intermediate code) that can run on any Java Virtual Machine (JVM), regardless of computer architecture.

2.5 Library Routines

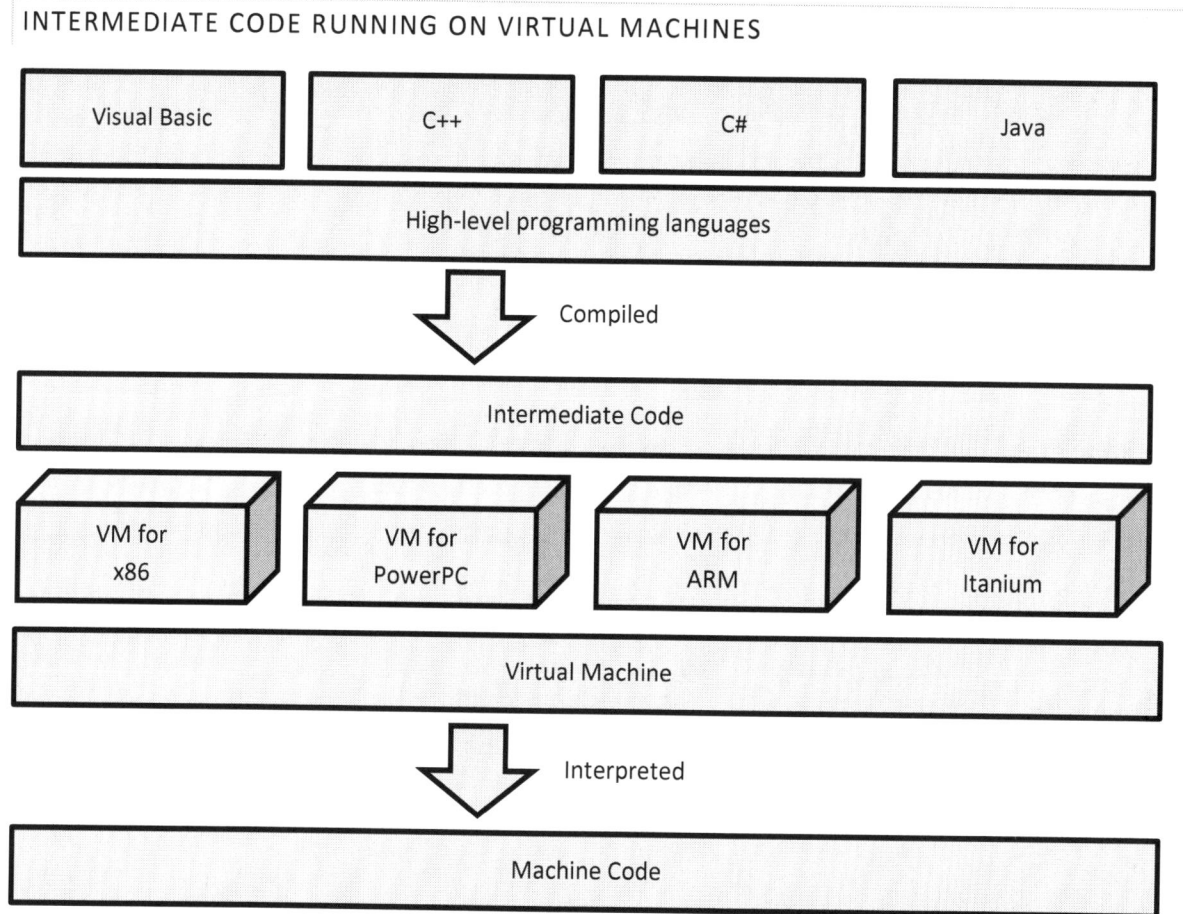

2.5 LIBRARY ROUTINES

Library routines are pre-compiled modules available for use by other programs.

- Programs are made up of **modules**
- Commonly used modules can be **compiled and stored** ready for repeated use
- These modules are stored in a **library**
- They are called **library routines**

Windows uses libraries in the form of DLL files (dynamic link library).

> A library is a collection of resources used to develop software.

Because the variable names and memory addresses will be different from one use of the library to the next, two programs are needed at runtime or when an executable file is created:

A **loader** has the job of **loading all the modules into memory**.

A **linker resolves references** in the main program, known as links or symbols, to library routines. If a function in a library routine is called, the linker will match the call in the program with the function in the library routine.

- **Advantage:** libraries reduce the amount of code that needs to be written.
- **Disadvantage:** if a library routine is updated, programs using it may stop working if the interfaces between the modules change.

CHAPTER 3 COMPUTER ARCHITECTURES

3.1 VON NEUMANN ARCHITECTURE

- John Von Neumann introduced the idea of the **stored program**
    - Previously, data and programs were stored separately
    - He realised that they were indistinguishable and can use the **same memory**
- Von Neumann architecture uses a **single processor**
- It follows a linear sequence of **fetch-decode-execute**
- *This architecture is used by most modern computers*

Von Neumann architecture requires specific registers in the CPU:

Register	Use
PC – Program Counter	Keeps track of where to find the next instruction
MAR – Memory Address Register	Hold memory address of current instruction
CIR – Current Instruction Register	Holds actual instruction to be executed
MDR – Memory Data Register	Acts like a buffer between memory and CPU
Accumulator	Holds results from ALU

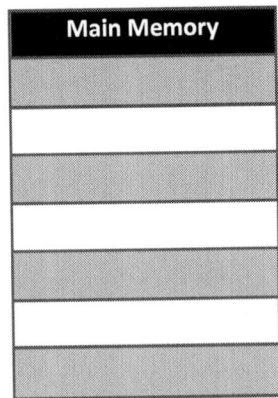
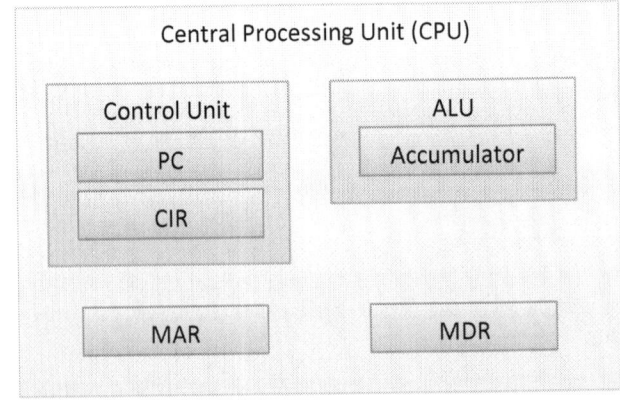

FETCH-DECODE-EXECUTE CYCLE

The **fetch-decode-execute cycle** is the process by which a computer retrieves an instruction from memory, determines what actions are required, and carries out those actions.

FETCH

- The **program counter (PC)** stores the address of the **next** instruction to be executed
- The program counter is **incremented** every time an instruction is accessed
    - It always points to the next instruction
- When the instruction is needed, the <u>address</u> is **copied** to the **memory address register** (MAR)
- The <u>instruction</u> stored in the memory location is then **copied** to the **memory data register**
- The <u>instruction</u> is then moved from the MDR to the **current instruction register**

DECODE

- The instruction held in the CIR is split into its separate parts
    - **Opcode** and **memory address** (operand)
- The memory address is placed in the **memory address register** and the data collected from it is placed in the **memory data register**
- The operation is decoded by referring to a **look up table**
    - This will give the control unit instructions about what needs to be done

EXECUTE

- The instruction is executed on the data held in the MDR.

The following is the algorithm showing all steps in the cycle.

1. Load the address in the PC into the MAR
2. Increment the PC by 1
3. Load the instruction that is in the memory address (given by the MAR) into the MDR
4. Load the instruction that is now in the MDR into the CIR
5. Decode the instruction in the CIR
6. If the instruction is a jump instruction then
    a. Load the address part of the instruction into PC
    b. Reset by going to step 1
7. Execute the instruction
8. Reset by going to step 1

The fetch-decode-execute cycle is repeated continuously by the CPU while the computer is running.

3.2 CO-PROCESSORS

A maths co-processor is a device that has a number of registers that are long enough to handle the length of floating point numbers in one go. This makes processing faster.

- Floating point numbers require significantly larger storage space as they are comprised of a long string of bits
- Being able to cope with the larger number in one go requires fewer calls to memory and hence speeds up processing

3.3 PARALLEL PROCESSING

PIPELINING

Rather than taking instructions through the fetch-decode-execute cycle one at a time, the processor can be split up into 3 parts, each handling 1 phase. This is called **pipelining**.

Fetch	Decode	Execute
Instruction 1		
Instruction 2	Instruction 1	
Instruction 3	Instruction 2	Instruction 1
Instruction 4	Instruction 3	Instruction 2
Instruction 5	Instruction 4	Instruction 3

- Each instruction is moved through the fetch-decode-execute cycle, but registers not in use are used to start the processing of the next instruction.
- Pipelining **increases the speed** of throughput while the pipes are kept full.

A problem occurs if the next instruction sequentially is not the one needed, i.e. if there is a **jump instruction**. For example, if instruction 3, in the example above, is a jump instruction to instruction 10, instructions 4 and 5 are no longer needed so the pipes will have to be cleared and the cycle restarted.

ARRAY PROCESSORS

- Array processors contain **multiple ALUs within a single processor**
- Good for **performing the same instruction on multiple items of data**
- Allows the **same calculation to be done on every element in an array** simultaneously
- Array processors are used in graphics cards when an instruction must be applied to every pixel

PARALLEL PROCESSORS

A system using parallel processors uses many independent processors working in parallel on the same program.

- **Speeds up processing by doing multiple things at the same time**
- **Programs have to be written specially for parallel processors**

E.g. a computer predicting the weather, where data from many sources needs to be processed simultaneously.

3.4 RISC AND CISC

Reduced instruction set computer and complex instruction set computer are two approaches to processor design.

- **RISC** has **simple hardware** and uses **more complex programming** to carry out tasks
- **CISC** uses **more complex hardware** to make **programming simpler**

CHAPTER 4 DATA REPRESENTATION

This section deals with the representation of numbers in a computer, specifically floating point binary.

4.1 EXPRESSING REAL NUMBERS IN BINARY

A **real** number is a **decimal number**, i.e. not a whole number.

Binary is a **base 2** number system. For example, the number eleven in binary is 1011:

$2^3 = 8$	$2^2 = 4$	$2^1 = 2$	$2^0 = 1$
1	0	1	1

Decimal numbers can be represented in binary by extending this table to the right of the decimal point.

- Consider the **real** number 11.375 in base 10. This is equal to $11\frac{3}{8}$.
- We already know that 11 = 1011.
- The $\frac{3}{8}$ is equal to $\frac{1}{4} + \frac{1}{8}$ so the number 11.375 can be represented as 1011.0110:

$2^3 = 8$	$2^2 = 4$	$2^1 = 2$	$2^0 = 1$		$2^{-1} = \frac{1}{2}$	$2^{-2} = \frac{1}{4}$	$2^{-3} = \frac{1}{8}$	$2^{-4} = \frac{1}{16}$
1	0	1	1	.	0	1	1	0

4.2 NEGATIVE NUMBERS IN BINARY

The two methods of representing negative numbers in binary were covered in F451:

- Sign and magnitude
- Two's complement

SIGN AND MAGNITUDE

Sign and magnitude is one method of representing negative numbers in binary. The first bit is used as a 'plus or minus' sign. <u>0 is used for a positive number and 1 for negative.</u>

- The most significant bit represents the **sign**
- The remaining bits indicate the **magnitude**

Chapter 4 Data Representation

TWO'S COMPLEMENT

Another method of representing a negative number in binary is **two's complement**. In this system, the **most significant bit** (the first, left-most bit) has a **negative** value.

-8	4	2	1

Values are added as normal. The lowest binary number in a 4-bit integer would be 1000 = -8, and the highest would be 0111 = 7. Therefore an N-bit, two's complement system can represent every integer in the range (-2^{N-1}) to $(2^{N-1} - 1)$.

To write a negative number in two's complement form, **flip and add one**:

1. Write the number in binary as though it were positive (the modulus of the number)
2. Flip each bit – replace each '0' with a '1' and vice versa
3. Add one to the result

For example, to write -6 in binary, using two's complement, first write 6 in binary: 0110; then flip each bit: 1001; and then add one: 1010. We can confirm this using the table above: -8 + 0 + 2 + 0 = -6.

The advantage of two's complement is that **addition and subtraction are easier**:

- Addition is more straightforward because negative numbers can be added to positive numbers with normal binary addition.
- This consequently makes subtraction more straightforward. For example, '5 subtract 3' is the same as '5 add -3'. The -3 can be represented with two's complement and the two numbers added.

HOW IT WORKS - *Not in the spec but interesting nonetheless.*

If we work with a 4-bit integer using two's complement, the highest positive value we can represent is seven. If we add one to this byte, we get the following:

```
  0111
+ 0001
======
  1000
```

1000, in our two's complement system, is of course negative eight, so we can see that the numbers 'wrap around'. That is, if we add one to the highest number, we get the lowest number.

We can therefore imagine the number line to be circular, as shown to the right. The dotted line shows the separation between positive and negative numbers.

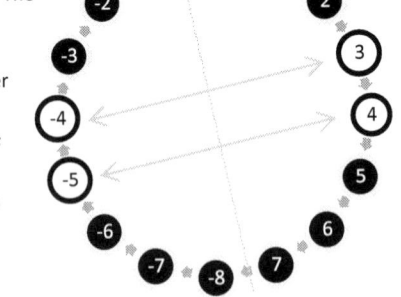

When we apply the bitwise NOT to a number in the circle (i.e. flip each bit), we get the number opposite through the line of separation. This will yield the one's complement of the number E.g. flipping the bits in 4 (0100) will give -5 (1011). The same with 3 and -4. *This process comes from subtracting the number from 2^N-1*. You will notice that applying this operation achieves the same effect as multiplying the number by -1 and subtracting 1. If we are making the two's complement of a number, we only want to multiply it by -1 so we add 1 to correct the error, hence, 'flip and add one'.

When we add a negative number to a positive number, the correct answer arises due to modular arithmetic. Consider -3+4 which, in binary, would be 1101 + 0100. If we briefly ignore two's complement, this binary addition is the same as 13+4, which is 17. If you start at zero in the diagram and count round 17 places, you'll find you end up at 1, which is the answer to -3+4.

Similarly, -4+3 would be 1100+0011. Again, the processor would add these as though they were the numbers 12 and 3, which would be 15. Counting round 15 in the diagram yields the result -1, which is correct.

This 'counting round' is known as modular arithmetic. Like a clock face, numbers repeat once the modulus is reached.

4.3 FLOATING POINT BINARY

Floating point numbers increase the range of numbers that a computer can store.

The number 11.375 can be written as 0.11375×10^2 in decimal (base 10). If we always write numbers in the same form, all we need to store are the numbers 0.11375 and 2.

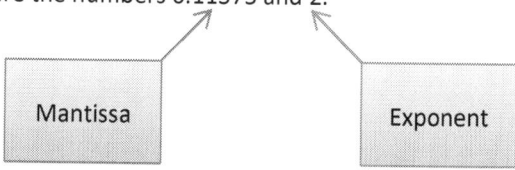

This notation can be applied to binary numbers (base 2)...

The number 11.375 can be represented as 1011.0110 in binary. This is the same as 0.10110110×2^4.

Obviously we're mixing binary with denary here, but it's a power of 2 because binary is base 2 – each column is only 2 times bigger than the one to its right, as opposed to 10 times bigger in denary.

Again, sticking to the same form, that is, the decimal point would appear after the first bit, all we need to store is 01011011 and 4, which would be 0100 in binary:

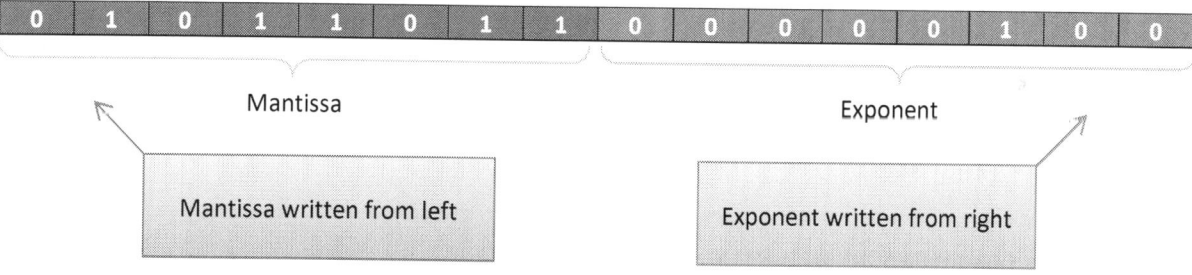

Sometimes we need a negative exponent so the **exponent is always in two's complement form**. If the number we're representing is negative, the mantissa is also in two's complement form. Care must be taken when representing a negative number, though, as explained on the next page.

NORMALISING A REAL BINARY NUMBER

The mantissa is said to be normalised if the first two digits are different.

- With a positive number, move the decimal point until the first '1' is immediately to the **right** of it.
- **The first two digits of a normalised positive number are '01'.**

Care must be taken when normalising a negative number:

1. Normalise the positive version of the number
2. Find the two's complement of the whole mantissa

E.g. the number -11:

- Represent the positive version
    - $11_{10} = 1011$
    - Normalise: 0.1011×2^{100}

| 0 | 1 | 0 | 1 | 1 | 0 | 0 | 0 | 0 | 0 | 0 | 0 | 0 | 1 | 0 | 0 |

- Find the two's complement of the mantissa (flip and add one)

| 1 | 0 | 1 | 0 | 1 | 0 | 0 | 0 | 0 | 0 | 0 | 0 | 0 | 1 | 0 | 0 |

If you move the decimal point according to the exponent, you get 10101, which is -11 using two's complement.

- **The first two digits of a normalised negative number are '10'**

TRADE-OFF BETWEEN ACCURACY AND RANGE

- There is a finite number of bits that can be used to represent a number in a computer.
- If more bits are used for the mantissa, less must be used for the exponent.

If we consider this in denary:

Suppose we used only 1 digit for the mantissa, but 5 for the exponent. The biggest number we can represent is 9×10^{99999}. On the other hand, if we used 5 digits for the mantissa but only 1 for the exponent, the biggest number would be 9.9999×10^9. This is far smaller but much more accurate because of the extra decimal places; we can keep more digits in the mantissa before rounding off.

- **Large range = low accuracy**
- **Small range = high accuracy**

CHAPTER 5 DATA STRUCTURES AND DATA MANIPULATION

This section covers types of data structure, sorting and searching algorithms, and the method of merging data.

5.1 DATA STRUCTURES

- A **static** data structure is one that does not change in size while the program is running
- A **dynamic** data structure can change size while the program is running

	Static Data Structure	Dynamic Data Structure
Advantages	<ul><li>Compiler can allocate space during compilation</li><li>Easy to program</li><li>Easy to check for overflow</li><li>An array allows random access</li></ul>	<ul><li>Only uses the space needed at the time</li><li>Makes efficient use of memory</li><li>Storage no longer required can be returned to the system for other uses</li></ul>
Disadvantages	<ul><li>Programmer has to estimate the maximum amount of space that is going to be needed</li><li>Can waste a lot of space</li></ul>	<ul><li>Difficult to program</li><li>Can be slow to implement searches</li><li>A linked list only allows serial access</li></ul>

STACK

A **stack** is a **last-in-first-out** (**LIFO**) data structure. It is a *dynamic* data structure that can only be accessed at one end, like a <u>stack of plates in a cafeteria</u>.

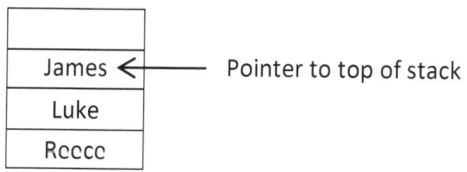

Pointer to top of stack

When items are removed from the stack, only the pointer is adjusted. This means that data is not deleted until it is overwritten by new data.

Operations that can be performed on a stack:

- **Push** – *add an item to the top of the stack*
- **Pop** – *remove an item from the top of the stack*
- **Top** – *identify the item at the top of the stack (without removing it)*

PUSH ALGORITHM

1. Check to see if stack is full
2. If the stack is full, report error and stop
3. Increment the stack pointer
4. Insert new data item into cell pointed to by the stack pointer and stop

POP ALGORITHM

1. Check to see if stack is empty
2. If the stack is empty, report error and stop
3. Copy data item from top of stack
4. Decrement the stack pointer and stop

Although the stack is a dynamic data structure, it cannot grow indefinitely. If it becomes too large, a **stack overflow** occurs.

Chapter 5 Data Structures and Data Manipulation

QUEUE

A **queue** is a **first-in first-out** (**FIFO**) data structure; new elements are added to the rear of the queue and elements leave from the front of the queue.

- A queue uses **two pointers**
    - One to the front of the queue
    - One to the rear of the queue

*This type of queue is called a double-ended queue, abbreviated deque (pronounced deck). This is only one implementation of a queue; another implementation is a **linked list**.*

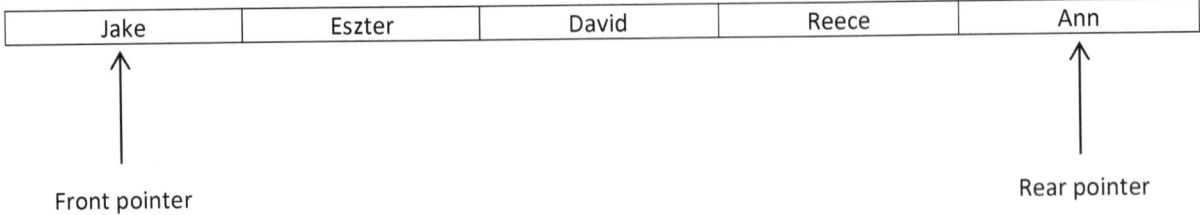

Operations that can be performed on a queue:

- **Push/Enqueue** – *add an item to the end of the queue*
- **Pop/Dequeue** – *remove an item from the front of a queue*
- **Front** – *identify the item at the front of the queue (without removing it)*

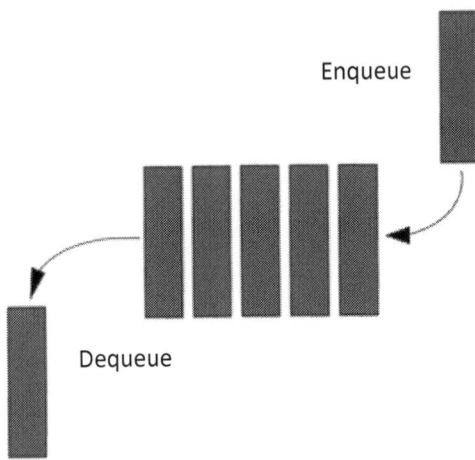

PUSH/ENQUEUE ALGORITHM

1. Check to see if queue is full
2. If the queue is full, report error and stop
3. Allocate memory to new node
4. Adjust the rear pointer to locate the new node

POP/DEQUEUE ALGORITHM

1. Check to see if queue is empty
2. If the queue is empty, report error and stop
3. Mark the memory that the node used as free
4. Adjust the front pointer to locate the previous node

BINARY TREE

A **binary tree** is a *dynamic* data structure that describes the relationship between data items.

- Each node has at most two child nodes
- Nodes with children are parent nodes
- The first node is called the **root node** (it has no parent)
- Siblings are nodes that share the same parent node

CONSTRUCTING AN ORDERED BINARY TREE

1. Place the first item at the **root**
2. Take each subsequent item in turn
3. Start at the root
    a. If the item is **less** than the root, branch to the **left**
    b. If the item is **greater** than the root, branch to the **right**
4. Apply step 3 to every node encountered

For example, consider the following list:

Philip, Dillon, Charles, Thomas, Lillian.

- First, we take Philip and make it the root node.
- Dillon is less than Philip (alphabetically), so we branch to the left.
- Charles is less than Philip, so we branch to the left.
    - Then we encounter Dillon; Charles is less than Dillon so we branch left again.
- Thomas is greater than Philip so we branch right.
- Finally, Lillian is less than Philip and then greater than Dillon so we branch left and then right.

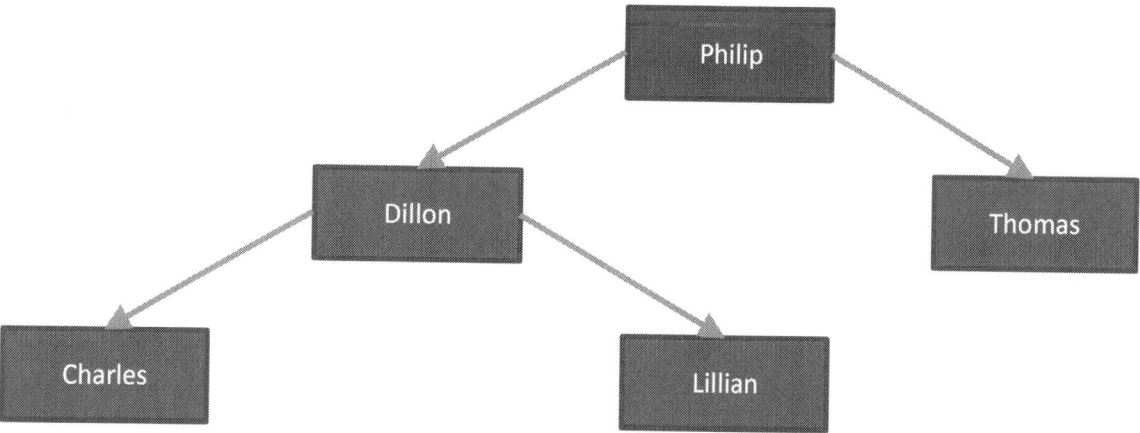

TRAVERSING A BINARY TREE

'Traversing a tree' means visiting each node of the tree in turn and performing some action on its contents – e.g. reading it. *A tree may be traversed in any of three ways:* **pre-order**, **in-order** *and* **post-order**. *The prefixes pre-, in- and post- refer to the point at which the root is visited. The left node is always visited before the right node.*

Consider this tree consisting of only three nodes:

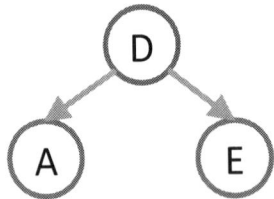

PRE-ORDER TRAVERSAL

- Visit the root node
- Traverse the left subtree
- Traverse the right subtree

The nodes are visited in the order D A E.

IN-ORDER TRAVERSAL

- Traverse the left subtree
- Visit the root node
- Traverse the right subtree

The nodes are visited in the order A D E ← *in ascending order*.

POST-ORDER TRAVERSAL

- Traverse the left subtree
- Traverse the right subtree
- Visit the root node

The nodes are visited in the order A E D.

These algorithms are recursive and can also be applied to larger trees.

DELETING A NODE

Simply deleting a node could detach child nodes from the tree. To avoid such disruption, a node is usually **marked as deleted** but left in the tree to maintain the structure. The traversal algorithms would skip nodes marked as deleted.

Alternatively, all data (except the node to be deleted) could be copied to a new tree.

IMPLEMENTING A BINARY TREE

To hold a tree structure in memory, a multi-dimensional array is used.

One column holds the name of the node while the others hold the left and right pointers.

The tree from page 29 would be held in an array similar to the following.
A pointer set to zero indicates a null node, i.e. the node has no child node on that side.

	Name	Left Pointer	Right Pointer
1	Philip	2	4
2	Dillon	3	5
3	Charles	0	0
4	Thomas	0	0
5	Lillian	0	0

It is also necessary to specify the **index** of the root node. In this case, the root node is Philip with index 1.

5.2 SORTING ALGORITHMS

There are many algorithms to put a list in order; insertion sort and quicksort are the two in the OCR spec.

INSERTION SORT

This is called 'shuttle sort' in OCR Decision Maths.

Insertion sort has a very simple algorithm. Essentially, **each element from the list is taken in turn and placed in the correct position in the sorted part of the list**.

This is done by looking at each element and comparing it with the previous elements.
It is moved to the left until its correct position is found, i.e. when a smaller element is encountered.

Consider the list {3, 7, 4, 9}. *In each step, the item under consideration is bold and underlined, and the items being compared are shaded.*

3	7	4	9	Nothing with which to compare 3
3	**7**	4	9	7 is compared with 3; no swap necessary
3	7	**4**	9	4 is compared with 7, 4 < 7 so 4 is moved
3	**4**	7	9	4 is compared with 3; no swap necessary
3	4	7	**9**	9 is compared with 7; no swap necessary

Insertion sort is most similar to the way in which a human would sort a hand of playing cards, for example.

The worst case input is an array sorted in reverse order with performance $O(n^2)$. However, the average case performance is also $O(n^2)$ making it impractical for long lists.

QUICKSORT

Quicksort is more efficient for sorting a large quantity of items. *Average case performance is O(n log n) although worst case is still $O(n^2)$.*

It works by picking an arbitrary **pivot** and moving everything lower than it to one side and everything greater than it to the other side. This will put the pivot in its <u>correct final position</u>. This gives us two unsorted sub-lists (the lower elements and the greater elements). These are sorted individually using the same algorithm making quicksort **recursive**.

The algorithm:

1. Pick an element, from the list, called the **pivot**
2. Reorder the list so that elements with values less than the pivot come before it and elements with values greater than the pivot come after it
3. Recursively sort the sub-list of lesser elements and the sub-list of greater elements

For example, consider the list {5, 2, 7, 1, 8, 6}.
First, we would pick a pivot. Usually, the first number is chosen as the pivot.
The list would be reordered so that everything lower than the pivot would come before it and everything greater would come after it. This would give us:

1 2 **5** 7 8 6.

We would then apply the same algorithm to the lists {1, 2} and {7, 8, 6}.

With the list {1, 2}, '1' would be the pivot. This would give us the sub-list of greater elements {2} which, when sorted, would obviously just return {2}.

When sorting the list {7, 8, 6}, '7' would be chosen as the pivot giving us:

> A list can have any number of elements including zero or one.

6 **7** 8,

resulting in the lists {6} and {8} which, again, would return themselves when sorted.

When every call to the function returns a sorted list, the result is {1, 2, 5, 6, 7, 8}.

MOVING ITEMS TO THE CORRECT SIDE OF THE PIVOT

Once a pivot has been chosen, items must be moved to the correct side of it, depending on whether they are greater or smaller than the value of the pivot. This is done by using **two pointers**; one starts at the beginning of the list, on the pivot, while the other starts at the end of the list.

The pointer locations on the list {5, 2, 7, 1, 8, 6}, where 5 is the pivot, will be as follows.

<u>5</u>	2	7	1	8	**6**
→					←

The pointer on the left will stay with the pivot (this will be underlined). The pointer on the right will make its way towards the pivot.

We compare the two numbers that are being pointed to (5 and 6, currently) and swap them if they're in the wrong order. The second pointer will then move one place towards the pivot.

<u>5</u>	2	7	1	**8**	6	
→				←		
<u>5</u>	2	7	**1**	8	6	*Swap*
→			←			
1	2	7	<u>5</u>	8	6	
→			←			
1	**2**	7	<u>5</u>	8	6	
	→		←			
1	2	**7**	<u>5</u>	8	6	*Swap*
		→	←			
1	2	<u>5</u>	7	8	6	
		→	←			
1	2	<u>5</u>	7	8	6	

This is where we take the lists {1, 2} and {7, 8, 6} and recursively sort them as described previously.

5.3 SEARCHING ALGORITHMS

The OCR spec covers two algorithms for locating an element in a list: serial search and binary search.

SERIAL SEARCH

A serial search looks through every element in order until the item is found or the end of the list is reached.

- A serial search is **easy to implement** because of its simplicity
- It has **good performance with very small lists** (less than 20)
- The **list does not need to be in order**

The worst case input for a serial search algorithm is one in which the item to be found is at the end of the list. In this case, n comparisons must be made, where n is the number of elements in the list. This gives a serial search a worst case performance of O(n), which makes it **slow for large lists**.

BINARY SEARCH

A binary search takes an **ordered list**. It decides whether the search item is higher or lower than the middle element of the list. It then focuses on the relevant half of the list and repeats the process.

1. Find the **middle** element
2. If it matches the search input, return its position
3. If it is **greater** than the search item, apply binary search to the sub-list to the left
4. If it is **lower** than the search item, apply binary search to the sub-list to the right

For example, if we had the list {1, 2, 4, 6, 7, 8, 9} and we were trying to locate 7, we'd start by finding the middle item...

1	2	4	**6**	7	8	9	7 is higher than 6
7	8	9					Apply binary search to right-hand sub-list. 7 is less than 8.
7							This gives us the one item list {7}. When we look for the middle value, we'll find our search item.

With each test that fails to find the search item at the middle position, the search is continued with a sub-list at most **half the size**. If we had a list with 8 elements, worst case would involve splitting it once into sub-lists of size 4, again into sub-lists of size 2, and a third time into sub-lists of size 1.

The following table shows the number of times a list must be halved, before a single element sub-list is reached, for different size lists.

Size of list	Number of divisions
2	1
4	2
8	3
16	4
32	5

Notice that:
$2^1 = 2$
$2^2 = 4$
$2^3 = 8$
$2^4 = 16$
$2^5 = 32$

For a list containing N elements, the worst case would involve $\log_2(N) + 1$ iterations. This is much better than serial search for large lists but remember that the list must be sorted first which might make it slower.

5.4 MERGING DATA

Quite often, data held in two separate files needs to be merged together. To merge two sorted lists, we **compare the first element** of each list and **move the smaller one to a new list**. This step is repeated on what remains of the two lists. Once one list becomes empty, the rest of the other list is appended to the new list.

Consider the two sorted lists:
{2, 4, 7, 10, 15} **and** {3, 5, 12, 14, 18, 26}

To merge these lists, we start by comparing 2 and 3. 2 is smaller so this is moved to the new list...

New List									Lists Being Merged					
									2	4	7	10	15	
									3	5	12	14	18	26
2									**4**	7	10	15		
									3	5	12	14	18	26
2	3								**4**	7	10	15		
									5	12	14	18	26	
2	3	4							**7**	10	15			
									5	12	14	18	26	
2	3	4	5						**7**	10	15			
									12	14	18	26		
2	3	4	5	7					**10**	15				
									12	14	18	26		
2	3	4	5	7	10				**15**					
									12	14	18	26		
2	3	4	5	7	10	12			**15**					
									14	18	26			
2	3	4	5	7	10	12	14		**15**					
									18	26				
2	3	4	5	7	10	12	14	15						
									18	26				
2	3	4	5	7	10	12	14	15	18					
									26					
2	3	4	5	7	10	12	14	15	18	26				

In practice, you wouldn't actually remove the smallest element in each iteration from the input list, you'd just increment a pointer that points to the items being compared.

Merge sort works by recursively breaking down a list of N elements into N lists of one element and then merging them together using the above algorithm. It was invented by John Von Neumann in 1945 and has a worst case performance of O(n log n) making it usually more efficient than quicksort and insertion sort but the OCR spec doesn't cover it.

CHAPTER 6 HIGH-LEVEL LANGUAGE PROGRAMMING PARADIGMS

A programming paradigm is a method or style of programming.

The programming paradigms you must know about are:

- Low-level
- Object-oriented
- Declarative
- Procedural

} These are examples of high-level languages

An assembly language is a low-level paradigm [see *The Function and Purpose of Translators*].

6.1 LOW VS. HIGH-LEVEL LANGUAGES

The 'low' and 'high' refer to the **amount of abstraction** between the language and machine code.

In a low-level language (an assembly language), the code has a **one-to-one relationship** with machine code and has a low level of abstraction.

A high-level language, such as Visual Basic, is **closer to English** and therefore has a high level of abstraction. It is 'further away' from the machine code and must be translated.

6.2 PROCEDURAL LANGUAGES

Procedural languages specify, exactly, the steps required to solve a problem. These languages use procedures (also known as subroutines), constructs, selection and repetition.

- A procedure is a list of statements/instructions with the aim of achieving a specific task
- Procedural programming is also known as **imperative** programming
- Constructs common to procedural languages (If-then statements, etc.) were covered in F452

6.3 DECLARATIVE LANGUAGES

A declarative language is one that describes what computation should be performed but not how to do it.

*It's a programming paradigm that <u>expresses the logic of a computation without describing its control flow</u>. This type of programming is based on **predicate logic**, which is a branch of mathematics that manipulates logical statements that can be either true or false.*

- A program will consist of a number of facts and rules about a particular subject
- Statements may be written in any sequence, making it easy to add new facts and rules
- Executing a program involves stating a goal to be achieved

Here is an example of some declarative programming.

```
cat (tom)
cat (leo)
cat (snowy)
mouse (jerry)
```
These are our **facts**: they define that Tom, Leo and Snowy are cats while Jerry is a mouse.

`chases (A, B) if cat (A) and mouse (B)`   This is a **rule**: A will chase B if A is a cat and B is a mouse.

We would then set a **goal**…

`chases (tom, jerry)?`

The process of finding the answer to a goal is called **satisfying the goal**. Of course, this goal would return true.

Suppose, instead, our goal were

`cat (X)?`

In this case, the program will return all values of X that would satisfy the goal.

1. Attempt to solve cat (X)
2. Find cat (tom)
3. Set X = tom
4. Attempt to solve cat (X)
5. Find cat (leo)
6. Set X = leo
7. Etc.

These are examples of instantiation. We say that X is instantiated to tom, etc. This is what happens when a solution to the goal is found.

After finding a solution to a goal, the program will go back and follow an alternative path to attempt to find another solution. After instantiating X to tom in step 3, step 4 is the same as step 1. This is called **backtracking**.

6.4 OBJECT-ORIENTED PROGRAMMING

Object-oriented programming (OOP) uses objects and classes.

- A class is a 'template' from which objects are created
- A class contains information that a typical object should have, as well as all of the methods it should have

Suppose a video game had a car – this would be an object. It is a specific example of the class *vehicle,* for example, which defines common features of all vehicles. The object would **inherit** the data and methods from this class.

Inheritance allows the re-use of code and the facility to extend the data and methods without affecting the original code. A class can inherit data and methods from its parent class and then add more data without affecting the original class. These classes are called **derived classes**.

Encapsulation is the concept that data in an object can only be accessed via the methods provided by the class.

UNIFIED MODELLING LANGUAGE (UML)

Unified Modelling Language is a set of diagrams used to represent object-oriented programs.

CLASS DIAGRAM

Object-oriented programming uses classes. A class contains the data about an object along with the methods through which the data can be accessed. A class can be drawn in a diagram.

Class Name
List of Attributes
List of Methods

For example, if we had a 'vehicle' class:

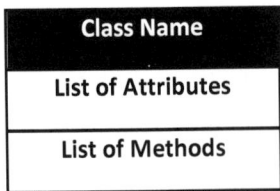

This is the name of the class

These are the attributes (the variables declared within the class) along with their data type. *Notice the colons.*

These are the methods that allow the data to be accessed.
The ellipsis shows that there are other methods that have not been listed.

Arrows are used to show inheritance. The Student and Teacher classes inherit everything from Personnel, and add more attributes and methods of their own.

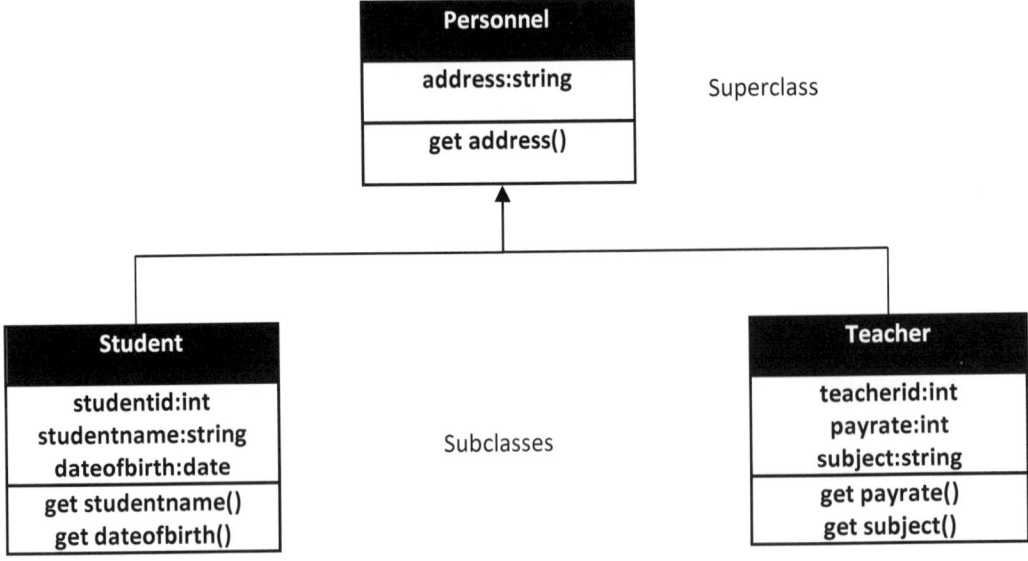

OBJECT DIAGRAMS

An object is an instance of a class and can also be represented by a diagram.

An **anonymous object** is one that represents any of the objects in the class, for example:

:Vehicle

Normally, however, an object diagram will represent a specific object…

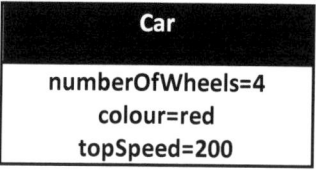

An object diagram shows the name of the object (not the class) and the values of the variables. *Notice that these data items have been inherited from the class but the values are specific to this instance.*

USE CASE DIAGRAMS

A use case diagram shows the functionality of a system rather than how things are done.

- Systems have users; in a use case diagram, they are called **actors**.
    - Actors are represented by **stick figures**.
    - There are two types of actor:
        - **Initiating actor** (teacher in example below)
        - **Receiving actor** (student in example below).
- The action is the use case and is represented on the diagram by an **oval**.
- Actors are linked to the oval by lines called **association lines.**
    - They show which actions are associated with which actors.

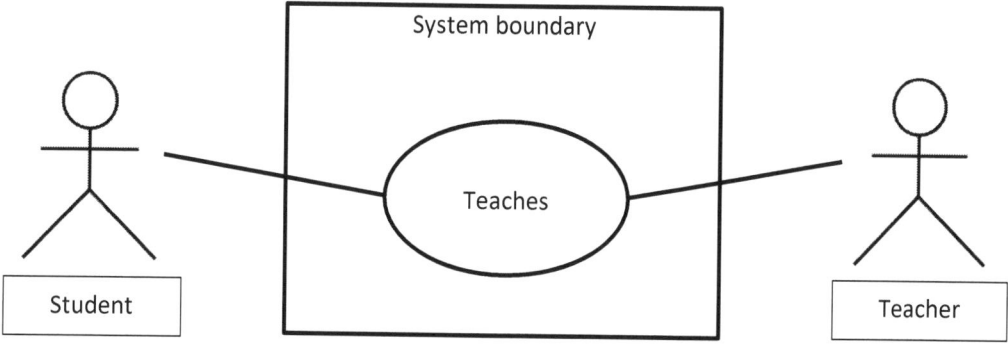

COMMUNICATION DIAGRAMS

Communication diagrams show how different objects work together to carry out a task.

- Each object is placed within a **rectangle** – *anonymous object*
- The objects are connected by **arrows**
    - The arrows show the **direction in which information flows**
    - The arrows are labelled with the **method used to access attributes of the objects**
    - They are also labelled with the **order in which each action happens**

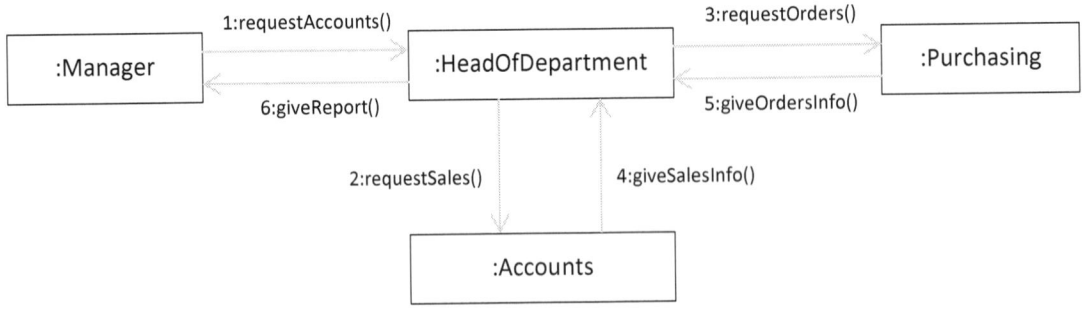

STATE DIAGRAMS

State diagrams show how an object might behave through the various processes of a system.

- Diagrams start with a **shaded circle to represent the initial state** of the system
    - This is known as the **entry point**
- Arrows are used to show **transitions between system states**
    - Transitions are brought about by events known as **triggers**
- The end of the system is represented by a **circle with a dot in it**
    - This is known as the **exit point**

This example shows the states of an employee.

In an exam, you have to be able to explain what's going on in a state diagram. In the example above:

- The first circle represents the entry point to the system
- The arrows represent the transitions to and from states
- The rounded rectangles represent the states in which the system can be
- The states themselves are 'working' and 'in meeting'
- The trigger is the event that changes the state of the system ('visitor arrives', in this case)
- The circle with a dot shows the exit point of the system

SEQUENCE DIAGRAMS

Sequence diagrams show how objects interact with each other over time.

- Each object has a dotted vertical line underneath it that shows how long that object exists in the process - this is known as the **lifeline**.
- These dotted lines sometimes become rectangles to show where the methods associated with the object are activated to do something.

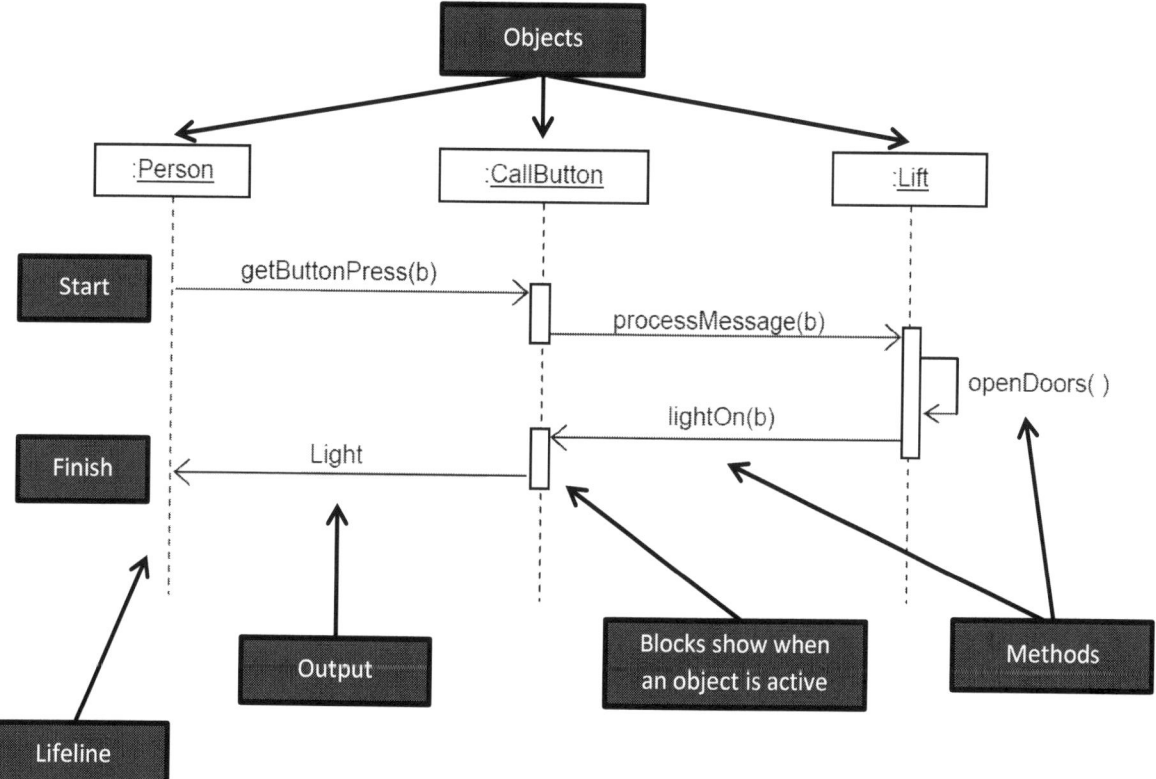

ACTIVITY DIAGRAMS

An activity diagram is just a flow chart.

You need to know what all of the symbols mean.

STANDARD SYMBOL SET

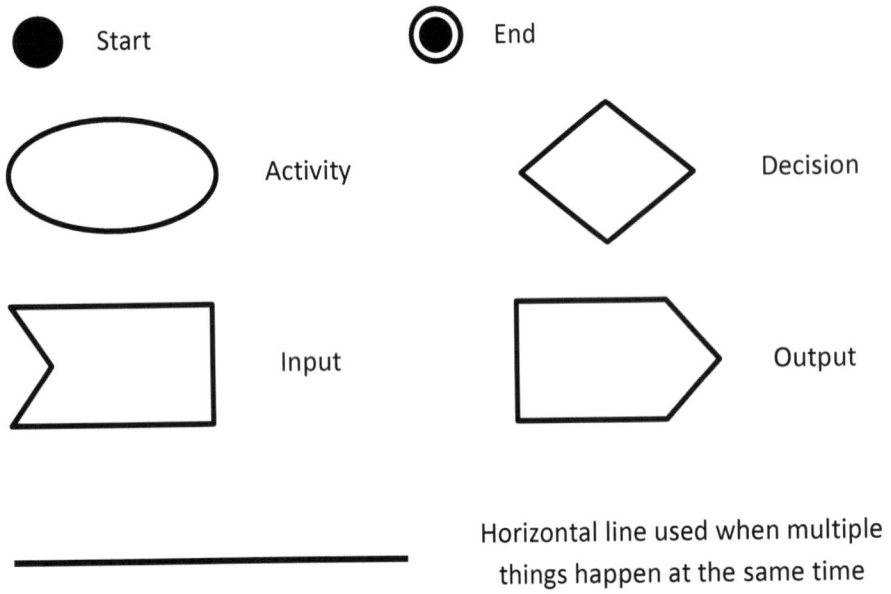

Horizontal line used when multiple things happen at the same time

SIMPLIFIED SYMBOL SET

A simplified set of symbols may be used.

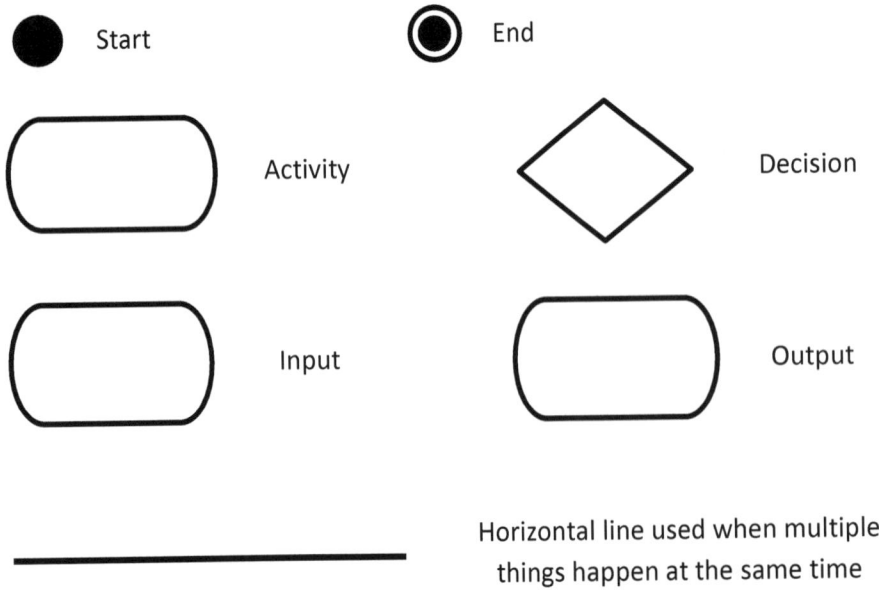

Horizontal line used when multiple things happen at the same time

Here is an example of an activity diagram with the standard symbol set.

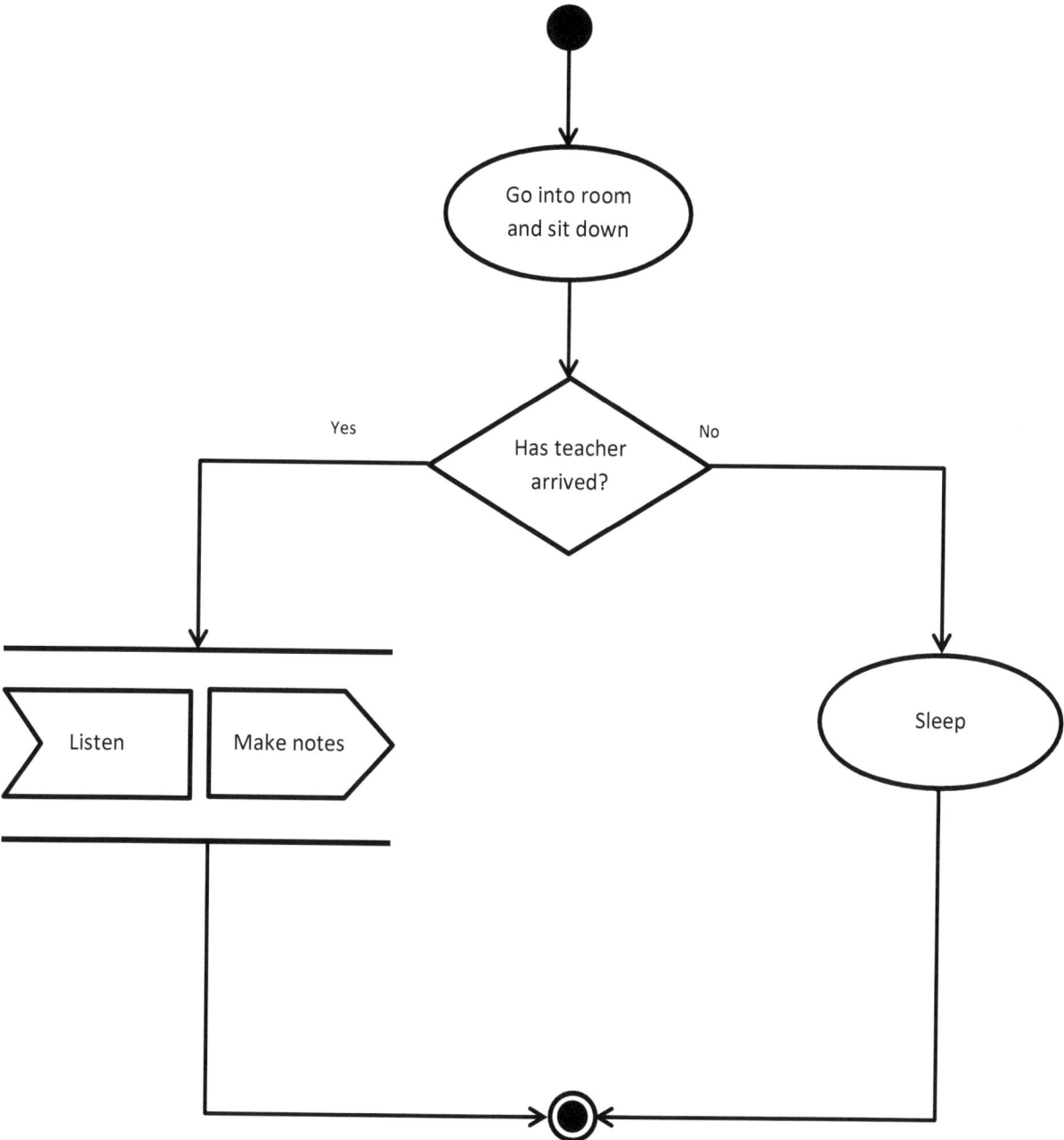

CHAPTER 7 PROGRAMMING TECHNIQUES

7.1 STEPWISE REFINEMENT

Stepwise refinement is the process of breaking a problem down into smaller and smaller sub-problems until they are simple enough to solve.

Stepwise refinement has the following advantages:

- Different people can work on different modules at the **same time**
- Modules can be allocated according to **expertise**
    - People can work on what they're good at
- Common modules can be **reused**
- **Testing is easier** to carry out on each module because they contain less code than the overall solution

7.2 STANDARD PROGRAMMING TECHNIQUES

- A **procedure** is a small section of code designed to carry out a specific task
- A **function** is a procedure that returns a single value
- **Parameters** are items of data passed to a procedure or function

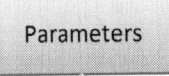

```
Function calculateArea(width, height) {
        area = width * height;
        return area;
}
```

A parameter can be passed *by value* or *by reference*.

- *By value* copies the actual value across to the subroutine so it can do whatever it likes to it without affecting the original variable.
- *By reference* gives the subroutine the memory address of the variable.

LOCAL AND GLOBAL VARIABLES

- A **local** variable exists only in the subroutine in which it is declared.
- A **global** variable can be used anywhere in the program.
- *If a variable is declared as both local and global, the local declaration will override the global one in that subroutine.*

USING A STACK TO HANDLE PROCEDURE CALLS

- A program can call procedures or functions
- These subroutines may also call another subroutine (or call themselves in recursive functions)
- The computer needs to know where to return to when the subroutine is completed
- A **stack** is used to keep track of this

When a subroutine is called, the return address is pushed onto a stack. This allows many 'layers' of subroutines to be handled at once. The parameters are also held in the stack.

7.3 BACKUS-NAUR FORM (BNF)

Backus-Naur Form (BNF) is an internationally accepted notation language to define the syntax of a system or programming language. **It is necessary to unambiguously define the syntax of a computer language.**

Suppose we wanted to define a digit using BNF.

Brackets < > mean 'can be defined further'

::= means 'is defined to be'

`<digit> ::= 0|1|2|3|4|5|6|7|8|9`

| means 'or'

We could then define an integer as follows.

`<integer> ::= <digit> | <digit><integer>`

This allows an integer to be a single digit or a digit followed by an integer. This part of the definition is recursive. It allows any number of digits.

Another example of BNF includes the definition of a staff code being entered into a database.

```
<DIGIT> ::= 0|1|2|3|4|5|6|7|8|9
<LETTER> ::= A|B|C|D|E
<STAFF_CODE> ::= <LETTER><DIGIT> | <STAFF_CODE><DIGIT>
```

This means a staff code can be a letter and then any number of digits.

D4, E644678 and A564 would all be valid staff codes.
The following examples would be invalid staff codes:

- Hf – because H is not defined to be a letter
- d4 – because a lowercase 'd' is not defined to be a letter
- A56E – because you can only have a letter at the beginning of a staff code
- AD574 – because the definition only allows a single letter at the beginning of a staff code

7.4 SYNTAX DIAGRAMS

Syntax diagrams are a diagrammatic way of representing a BNF definition.

The staff code example from above would be represented as follows.

LETTER:

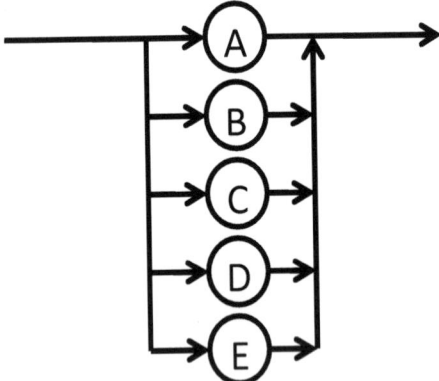

DIGIT:

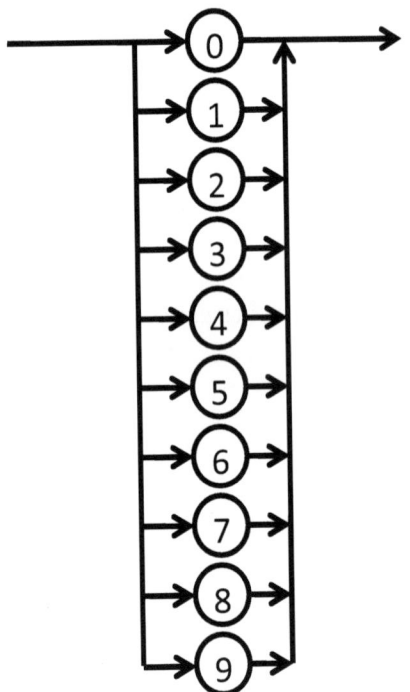

STAFF_CODE:

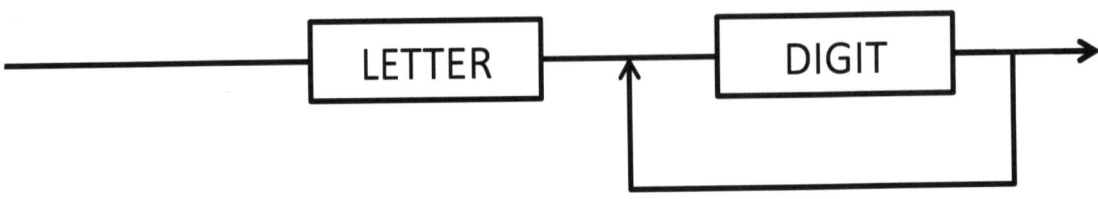

7.5 REVERSE POLISH NOTATION

Reverse Polish Notation is an unambiguous method of writing mathematical expressions without brackets.

- Adding two numbers is written as A + B
- This is called **infix** notation as the operator is in between the operands
- To multiply the result by two, we'd write 2 * (A + B)
- We need brackets to make sure it's done in the right order

Polish notation avoids brackets by putting each operator before its operands.
A + B would become +AB, and 2 * (A + B) becomes *2+AB

Reverse polish notation is simply polish notation written the other way around, so those examples would be AB+ and AB+2*. This can be read as 'take the numbers A and B and add them together, then take the result and the number 2 and multiply them together'.

Reverse polish notation puts each operator after its operands.

CONVERTING BETWEEN INFIX NOTATION AND REVERSE POLISH NOTATION

Binary tree diagrams can be used to convert between normal, infix notation and reverse polish notation.

- You must use **post-order traversal** of the tree to obtain **reverse polish notation**
- Using **in-order traversal** will obtain normal, **infix notation**.

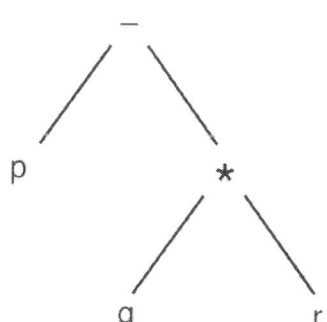

Using post-order traversal on this tree, we get pqr*-, which is the reverse polish. Alternatively, in-order traversal will give us the infix notation p-(q*r).

It is clear that each operator has two branches; each branch represents one of its operands. The subtraction has the operands p and the result of the right-hand sub-tree.

Stacks are also associated with reverse polish notation. They can be used to evaluate expressions using the following algorithm:

1. **Read** expression from left to right
2. If a **number** is encountered, **PUSH** it onto stack
3. If an **operator** is encountered, **POP** two numbers from stack and carry out operation
    a. **PUSH result** onto stack
4. End if last item in expression has been dealt with

The following example shows the algorithm when applied to the expression 6 4 5 + * 25 2 3 + / -.

5
4
6

The numbers 6, 4 and 5 are encountered so they are PUSHED onto the stack, one by one.

9
6

Then an operator is encountered: +.
The top two numbers are POPPED (4 and 5) and the operation is carried out on them.
The result is PUSHED onto the stack (9).

54

Another operator is encountered: *.
This is applied to the two items POPPED from the stack (9 and 6).
The result is PUSHED onto the stack.

3
2
25
54

The numbers 25, 2 and 3 are PUSHED onto the stack as they are encountered.

5
25
54

The '+' is encountered so the 3 and 2 are POPPED, added together, and the result is PUSHED (5).

5
54

The 5 and 25 are POPPED and divided *(notice the order of the operands)* and the result, 5, is PUSHED.

49

Finally, the 5 and 54 are POPPED and subtracted, and the result is PUSHED back onto the stack. This is our final answer. *Again, notice that the first operand to be POPPED is placed to the right of the operator, i.e. 54 – 5.*

CHAPTER 8 LOW-LEVEL LANGUAGES

See the section on *Assembly Language and Assemblers* on page 11 for more information on low-level languages. Some keywords are summarised below, though.

- **Opcode** – *codes which represent the operations that a computer can carry out*
- **Mnemonics** – *words to represent each opcode that a human can understand*
- **Operand** – *the data in an instruction on which the operator (opcode) is applied*
- **Address labels** – *symbolic representation of binary address codes for easier programming*

See *Chapter 3 Computer Architectures* for more information regarding CPU registers.

- **Program counter (PC)** – *keeps track of the location of the next instruction to be executed*
- **Memory address register (MAR)** – *holds the address of the instruction or item of data that is to be fetched from memory*
- **Current instruction register (CIR)** – *holds the instruction that is to be executed, ready for decoding*
- **Memory data register (MDR)** – *acts like a buffer between the registers and the memory*
- **Accumulator** – *temporarily holds results from ALU*

A **jump instruction** will tell the CPU to execute an instruction that is not sequentially next. A jump that is not dependent upon a condition being true is called an **unconditional jump**.

8.1 MEMORY ADDRESSING

An instruction in memory consists of an **opcode** and an **operand**. The operand is the data on which the operation should be applied. The method used to locate the data is known as **memory addressing**.

IMMEDIATE ADDRESSING

- This is sometimes called an **immediate operand**
- The value in the address part of the instruction is actually the value to be used
- Immediate addressing does not involve the memory at all

For example, if you wanted to add 3 to the contents of the accumulator, this would simply be:

$$\text{ADD} \quad 0011$$

Opcode
In our system, ADD is the mnemonic for adding to the contents of the accumulator.

Operand
0011 is the actual piece of data to which the operation is applied. 0011 is 3 in binary so 3 is added to the contents of the accumulator.

Disadvantages

- The data **cannot be used by other instructions**.
    - In our example, the value 3 would have to be repeated in every instruction that needs it.
- It is **difficult to change** the value.

DIRECT ADDRESSING

- **Direct addressing** points to a location in memory that holds the data.

ADD 0011

With direct addressing, this would mean 'go and find the data that is in memory address 3 and add it to the accumulator'.

The number of memory addresses that can be accessed is limited by the number of bits available for the operand. If the operand were a 16-bit number, 2^{16} memory locations can be addressed, giving us 64kB of memory, which isn't a lot.

INDIRECT ADDRESSING

- **Indirect addressing** points to a memory location that holds another memory location that holds the data to be used
- Useful because it allows access to **larger memory addresses.**

ADD 0011

This would now mean 'go to memory location 3 where you'll find another memory location; go to this other address and use the value found there.'

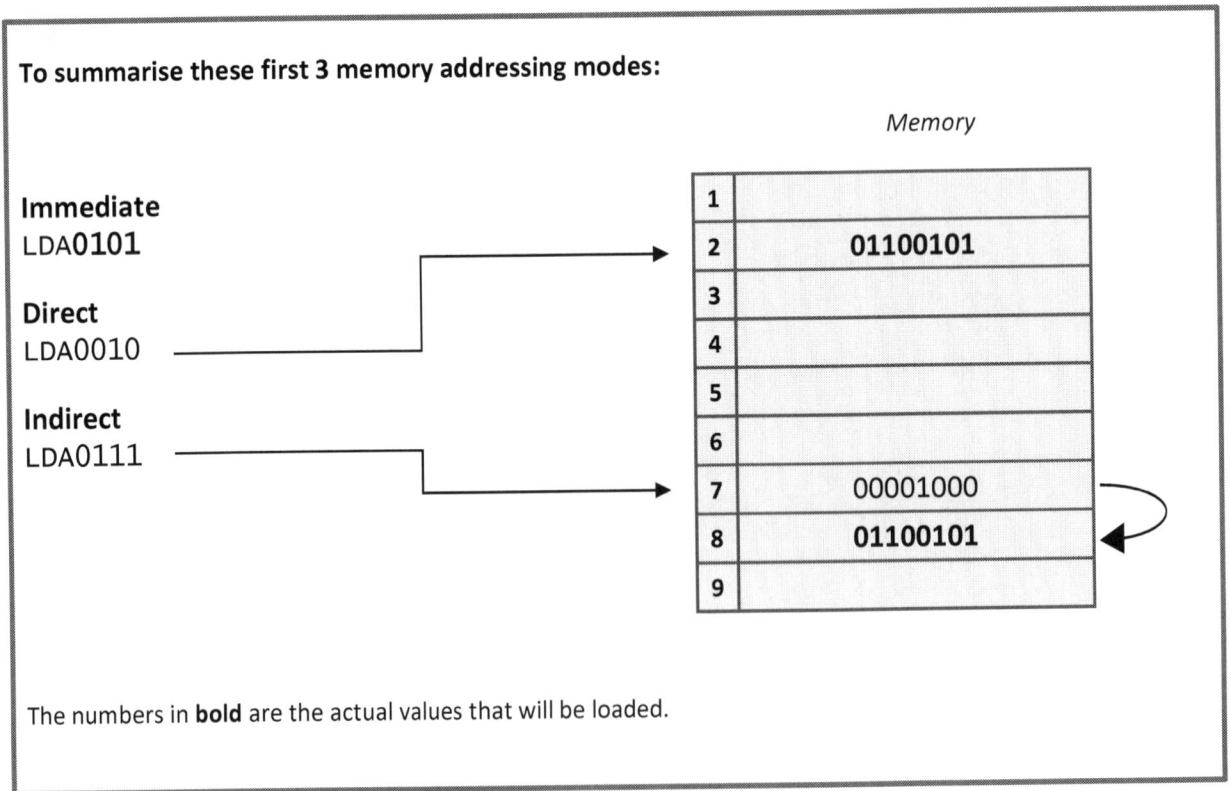

The numbers in **bold** are the actual values that will be loaded.

INDEXED ADDRESSING

- **Indexed addressing** uses a special register called the **index register**.
- The value of the index register is **incremented** each time it is referred to.
- The memory address given in the instruction is then **adjusted** according to the value of the register.
    - This means that the same instruction can be **repeated** but applied to a different memory location each time.
    - This is useful for processing an **array**, which would be stored in a contiguous block of memory.

For example, suppose we wanted to add up every number in an array. Normally, we would execute:

ADD 0001
ADD 0010
ADD 0011
etc.

However, every operator is the same (*ADD*), only the operand changes. This means that we could repeat the same instruction and use the index register to increment the memory address.

RELATIVE ADDRESSING

When we write a program, we don't know where in memory it will be held during execution, but we do know that it will go into memory as a single block. In relative addressing, **all memory addresses are relative to the first one.**

If the first instruction in a program is ADD 100, all subsequent addresses will be relative to 0100. This means that if the next instruction is ADD 010, the memory address that is accessed is 100+010=**110**.

CHAPTER 9 DATABASES

9.1 FLAT FILES DATABASES

A flat file database is a database consisting of a single table. The following is an example of a flat file.

Product	Price	Customer Name	Telephone	Date
Hedge Trimmer	£15.00	John	01746573425	10/06/11
Weed Killer	£4.99	Fred	09876453678	11/06/11
Weed Killer	£4.99	Jake	67654565457	12/06/11
Compost	£9.99	John	01746573425	15/06/11
Plant Pot	£3.00	John	01746573425	15/06/11

Storing all data in a single table has some advantages:

- All records are stored in the **same place**
- **Easy** to understand
- **Simple sorting and searching** of records – serially search until record is found
- Records can be viewed based on **simple criteria**

Suppose the purchasing department in a company keep a file containing product details, and the sales department keep a similar file to keep track of stock levels. If flat files are used, these two files will have no connection, and this will cause difficulties.

- Flat files lead to **data duplication** *(as seen above – e.g. the weed killer product appears twice)*
- Very **hard to update** details for a particular customer, for example
    - Every instance must be updated individually
    - If duplicate data appears in a separate file, this must be updated manually
- If a **new field** needs to be added, all programs using the file must be updated
    - The code to read a flat file will no longer work if the number of fields that it is programmed to read is changed
- Files are **incompatible** with a program if they are written using a different language/structure
- Each time a new query is needed, a **new program** must be written

To overcome these limitations, a **relational database** can be used.

9.2 RELATIONAL DATABASES

Instead of placing data in separate, unrelated files, it is stored in tables that are related to each other.

From the example on the previous page, three tables could be created, holding product details, customers and orders. This means <u>data is no longer duplicated</u>.

- Each table has a **key field**, or a **primary key**, which acts as an identifier
  - A primary key must be <u>unique</u>
- Tables can be linked to each other by using **foreign keys**
- Instead of fields, columns are called **attributes**
- Instead of records, rows are called **tuples**

The flat file database in the example above could be separated into the following relational tables:

CustomerID	CustomerName	Telephone
1	John	01746573425
2	Fred	09876453678
3	Jake	67654565457

ProductID	Product	Price
1	Hedge Trimmer	£15.00
2	Weed Killer	£4.99
3	Compost	£9.99
4	Plant Pot	£3.00

OrderID	CustomerID	ProductID	Date
1	1	1	10/06/11
2	2	2	11/06/11
3	3	2	12/06/11
4	1	3	15/06/11
5	1	4	15/06/11

This is *better* than the original flat file because customer and product details are **not duplicated**. However, notice that John bought compost and a plant pot at the same time. With this model, a second order must be created to allow a second product to be purchased.

The structure we want can be represented using an entity-relationship (E-R) diagram.

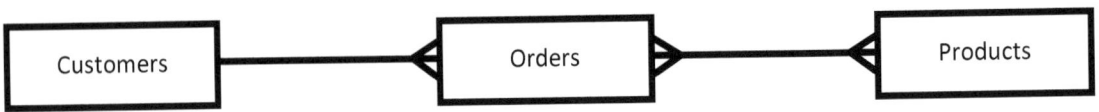

The problem outlined above arises as a result of the many-to-many relationship (between Orders and Products). **Many-to-many relationships are not allowed in databases**.

This can be resolved by adding another table, known as a **linking entity**.

Our tables are now structured as follow:

CustomerID	CustomerName	Telephone
1	John	01746573425
2	Fred	09876453678
3	Jake	67654565457

ProductID	Product	Price
1	Hedge Trimmer	£15.00
2	Weed Killer	£4.99
3	Compost	£9.99
4	Plant Pot	£3.00

OrderID	CustomerID	Date
1	1	10/06/11
2	2	11/06/11
3	3	12/06/11
4	1	15/06/11

OrderProductID	OrderID	ProductID
1	1	1
2	2	2
3	3	2
4	4	3
5	4	4

This is the linking table, which allows a single order to include multiple products.

9.3 DATABASE NORMALISATION

Normalisation is the process of efficiently organising data in a database. It has two goals:

- Eliminating **redundant data** - *storing the same data in more than one table*
- Ensuring data **dependencies make sense** - *only storing related data in a table*

There are different levels of normalisation. The ones to be aware of range from first normal form (1NF) to third normal form (3NF).

FIRST NORMAL FORM (1NF)

First normal form achieves the following:

- Eliminate **duplicative columns** from the same table
- Create **separate tables for each group of related data**, and identify each row with a unique column (the **primary key**)

SECOND NORMAL FORM (2NF)

Second normal form further addresses the concept of removing duplicative data:

- Meet all the requirements of the first normal form
- Remove subsets of data that apply to multiple rows of a table and place them in separate tables – i.e. **remove data that is duplicated within a table**
- Create relationships between these new tables through the use of **foreign keys**

THIRD NORMAL FORM (3NF)

Third normal form (3NF) goes one large step further:

- Meet all the requirements of the second normal form
- Remove transitive relationships – i.e. **remove columns that are not dependent upon the primary key** (and put them in new tables)

For example, if you had a table with the following fields:

- *Order Number (primary key)*
- *Customer Number*
- *Unit Price*
- *Quantity*
- *Total*

The customer number will depend upon the order number. The unit price and quantity are also dependent on a particular order. The total, however, is derived from the price and quantity, and can be calculated, therefore, it is not dependent upon the primary key and should not be stored in the table. It should be calculated 'on the fly'.

9.4 PRIMARY, SECONDARY AND FOREIGN KEYS

Although these terms have already been mentioned, you may get a question specifically asking about the purpose of these keys in a database.

PRIMARY KEY

The key used to **uniquely identify a tuple** (row) is called a primary key. *Include an example from the table in the question if asked about this.*

SECONDARY KEY

A secondary key is another attribute (field) which could have been the primary key.

If we had a table storing EmployeeID and NINumber, both would uniquely identify an employee so we say that they are **candidate keys**. If we choose EmployeeID as the primary key, NINumber would become the secondary key.

FOREIGN KEY

Foreign keys are used to link tables/create relationships between tables.

A primary key from one table is used as an attribute (field) in a second table to link them. In the second table, it is known as the foreign key.

9.5 DATABASE VIEWS

A view is the way in which a **user sees the data** and data structures in a database. A view consists of a stored query accessible as a virtual table. A view does not form part of the physical schema; it is a **dynamic, virtual table**.

- Views can represent a **subset of the data** contained in a table
- Views can **join and simplify** multiple tables into a single virtual table
- Views can **hide the complexity** of data
- Views can provide **extra security** by restricting the exposure of tables
    - This can be done by using passwords
    - It can also be achieved by checking the computer requesting data to make sure that the user is authorised to access it

9.6 DATABASE MANAGEMENT SYSTEMS

A database management system (DBMS) (or relational database management system) is a software package with the following facilities:

- Contains a **data definition language** (DDL) – allows tables to be defined (structure, data types, validation, etc.)
    - When a set of instructions in a DDL is compiled, the tables that are created are stored in a **data dictionary**
- Contains a **data manipulation language** (DML) – allows user to insert, update, delete, modify and retrieve data

The design of the tables and relationships within the database is called the **schema**.

THREE LEVEL DATABASE ARCHITECTURE

A database management system (DBMS) divides a database into three main levels.

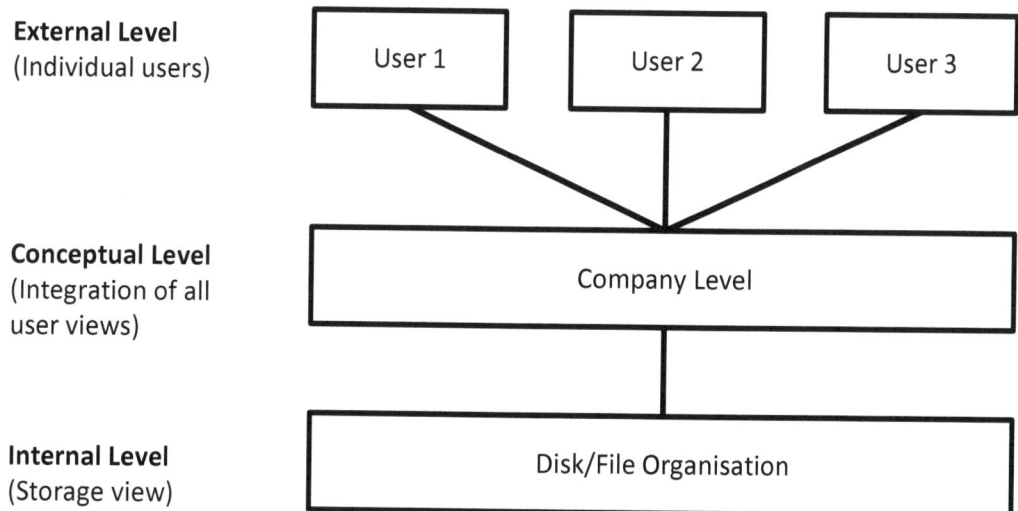

External Level (Individual users)

Conceptual Level (Integration of all user views)

Internal Level (Storage view)

EXTERNAL LEVEL
- The external level is concerned with the way in which **individual users see the data**
- Users will see the data through **views** (discussed above)

CONCEPTUAL LEVEL
- The conceptual level gives a **single, usable view** of all of the data in the database
- It is used mainly by the database **administrators**

INTERNAL LEVEL
- The internal level is a **low-level** representation of the database
- It is concerned with the way in which data is actually **stored** on disk
- This level is usually hidden by the database management system (DBMS)

APPENDIX 1 INDEX

abstraction 6, 36
accumulator 1, 20, 49
activity diagram 42
actors 39
algorithm 17, 21, 31, 32, 34, 35, 47, 48
analyser 14, 15
append 35
architecture 9, 11, 18, 20
array processor 22
assembler 11, 12
assembly language 11, 12, 36
attributes 53
backtracking 37
binary 10, 11, 17, 23, 24, 25, 29, 34, 49
binary search 34
BNF 15, 45, 46
boot 8
CIR 1, 20, 21, 49
CISC 22
class 37, 38, 39
cluster 9
code generation 13
code optimiser 16
command line 8
comments 14
communication diagram 40
compilation 10, 12, 13, 14, 16, 27
compiler 12, 13, 15, 16, 17, 18
conceptual level 57
constant 14, 17
co-processor 21
CPU 1, 8, 20, 49
data structure 1, 17, 27, 28, 29
DBMS 57
DDL 57
debugging 12
declaration check 15
declarative 36
decode 21
direct addressing 50
disk thrashing 6
DLL 19
DML 57
encapsulate 37
entity-relationship 54
execute 21
exit point 40
exponent 25, 26
external level 57
facts 36

FAT 9
fetch 20
fetch-decode-execute cycle 20
first come, first served 4
first normal form 55
flat file 52, 53
floating point 21, 25
flow of control 15
foreign key 53, 56
fragmentation 5, 9
function 19, 32, 44
global 17, 44
goal 36, 37
GUI 8
hardware 1, 8, 22
hardware error 1
hash table 17
hashing algorithm 17
high-level language 12, 18, 36
I/O bound 2
I/O interrupt 1
identifier 14, 17, 53
immediate addressing 49
imperative programming 36
indexed addressing 51
indexed Addressing 51
indirect addressing 50
inherit 37, 38
insertion sort 31
interface 1, 8
intermediate code 10, 16, 18
interpretation 10, 12
interpreter 12
interrupt 1, 7, 8
Java 18
jump 21, 22, 49
key field 53
keyword 12, 14
label 11, 49
label checks 15
lexeme 14
lexical analysis 13, 14
library 19
library routine 19
lifeline 41
linked list 9, 17, 27, 28
linker 19
linking entity 54
loader 8, 19
local 17, 44

lookup table	11, 16
low-level	36
machine code	10, 11, 12, 16, 18, 36
mantissa	25, 26
mapping	6
MAR	1, 20, 21, 49
MDR	1, 20, 21, 49
memory	1, 2, 3, 5, 6, 7, 8, 9, 11, 12, 16, 17, 19, 20, 21, 27, 28, 31, 44, 49, 50, 51
memory management	5
merging	27, 35
mnemonic	11, 49
multi-level feedback queue	4
node	28, 29, 30, 31
normalisation	55
normalise	26
object	10, 11, 12, 18, 37, 38, 39, 40, 41
object code	10, 11, 12, 18
object-oriented	37
opcode	11, 49
operand	49
operating system	1, 5, 8
optimisation	13, 16
OS	2, 3, 5, 8, 9
page file	6
paging	5, 7
parallel processing	22
parameter	44
PC	1, 8, 20, 21, 49
pipelining	22
pivot	32, 33
pointer	9, 17, 27, 28, 31, 33, 35
polish notation	47
POST	8
primary key	53, 55, 56
primary memory	6
procedural	36
procedure	36, 44
processor bound	2
program interrupt	1
programming paradigms	36
queue	1, 3, 4, 5, 7, 28
quicksort	32
RAM	6, 8, 9
range	26
recursive	30, 32, 45
regular expression	14
relational database	53
relative addressing	51
reverse polish notation	47
RISC	22
ROM	8
round robin	4
rules	14, 36
scheduler	3
scheduling	2, 4
schema	56, 57
searching	27, 52
second normal form	55
secondary key	56
segmentation	5, 7
semantic check	15
sequence diagram	41
serial search	34
shortest job first	4
shortest remaining time	4
shuttle sort	31
sign and magnitude	23
sorting	27, 32, 52
source code	10, 11, 12, 14, 16, 17, 18
spool queue	7
spooling	7
stack	1, 5, 27, 45, 47
state diagram	40
statements	36
stepwise refinement	44
symbol table	11, 14, 16, 17
synonym	17
syntax analysis	13, 15
syntax diagram	15, 46
table	9, 11, 14, 17, 21, 23, 24, 34, 52, 53, 54, 55, 56
third normal form	55
timer interrupt	1
time-slice	8
token	14
translate	11, 12, 16, 18
translator	10
traverse	30
tuples	53
two's complement	23
UML	38
use case	39
utility software	1
view	56, 57
virtual address translation	6
virtual addresses	6
virtual machine	10, 16, 18
virtual memory	6
Von Neumann	20, 35
whitespace	14

Printed in Great Britain
by Amazon.co.uk, Ltd.,
Marston Gate.